CONTENTS

YORK NOTES

Edward II

Christopher Marlowe

Note by Jill Barker

Jill Barker is hereby identified as author of this work in accordance with Section 77 of the Copyright, Designs and Patents Act 1988

YORK PRESS
322 Old Brompton Road, London SW5 9JH

PEARSON EDUCATION LIMITED
Edinburgh Gate, Harlow,
Essex CM20 2JE, United Kingdom
Associated companies, branches and representatives throughout the world

First published 2001

ISBN 0–582–43161–1

Designed by Vicki Pacey
Phototypeset by Gem Graphics, Trenance, Mawgan Porth, Cornwall
Colour reproduction and film output by Spectrum Colour
Produced by Addison Wesley Longman China Limited, Hong Kong

PART ONE

INTRODUCTION

HOW TO STUDY A PLAY

Studying on your own requires self-discipline and a carefully thought-out work plan to be effective. Read the entire play through more than once.

- Drama is a special kind of writing (the technical term is 'genre') because it needs a performance in a theatre to interpret its meaning fully. Try to imagine that you are a member of the audience when reading a play. Think about how it could be presented on the stage, not just about the words on the page. It will help you to form imaginative ideas about theatrical possibilities if you can see as many staged plays as possible – including more than one version of the one you are studying. If this is not possible, videos and cinema versions can be helpful.

- Drama is always about conflict of some sort (which may be below the surface, or within the mind of a character). Identify the conflicts in the play and you will be close to identifying the large ideas or themes which bind all the parts together.

- Make notes on **themes**, character, plot and any subplots. Include your own ideas here, and include similarities to other literary works you have read. This will make your responses more original and personal.

- Why do you like or dislike the characters in the play? How do your feelings towards them develop and change?

- Playwrights find nonrealistic ways of allowing an audience to see into the minds and motives of their characters, for example **soliloquy**, **asides** or musical cues to emotion. Consider how such dramatic devices are used in the play you are studying.

- Think of the playwright writing the play. Why were these particular arrangements of events, characters and speeches chosen?

- Cite exact sources for all quotations, whether from the text itself or from critical commentaries. Wherever possible find your own examples from the play to back up your *own* opinions.

- Always express your ideas in your own words.

This York Note offers an introduction to *King Edward II* and cannot substitute for close reading of the text and the study of secondary sources.

Edward II is much more than just a precursor to Shakespeare's history plays. It offers the reader an exciting roller-coaster ride through the ups and downs of Edward's lengthy reign (1307–27) compressed into twenty-five scenes. Twenty years are thus summarised in a stage work that lasts about three hours. The energy created by this compression sweeps us from one end of England to another, from joy and victory to defeat, despair and a grisly death. In reading *Edward II* or watching it performed we need to be prepared for its strongly homosexual element. The early twenty-first century with its liberal attitudes is perhaps the best moment we could possibly have to read the play without an excessive reaction to this element. Previous scholars certainly found it embarrassing, even scandalous, and tended to focus too intensely on that aspect of the play. Instead we should see Edward's sexual orientation as a context within which the play functions and not as a dominating issue in itself. The lords are seriously shocked by Edward's expenditure and by his favouring persons of a humbler class. They seem less troubled by the king's sexuality.

Marlowe offers us a self-willed, even foolish hero who seems difficult to like at first, but for whom we feel intense compassion by the conclusion of the play. We discover an **ambivalence** towards Edward in ourselves, and that brings with it an understanding of the rebels' position. The play does not just explain the problems of regicide, it causes the audience to experience both sides of the argument for and against Edward's kingship. The rebels too turn out to be less than admirable. The play reveals personalities in relation to (and clashing with) social institutions, especially the monarchy, but also marriage, parenthood and friendship.

Marlowe's language in *Edward II* is direct and readable, pushing the narrative forward in an economical style where every word counts. The occasional lyrical passages (such as Gaveston's speeches in Scene 1) are therefore especially striking and display verbally the difference in tone between the dynamic nobles and the hedonistic court. Speaking of Marlowe's poetic skill, Ben Jonson famously used the phrase 'Marlowe's mighty line' to describe his use of **blank verse**: a strongly rhythmic, regular unrhymed line in **iambic pentameter** which is usually (but not invariably) **end-stopped**. This later became the basis of Shakespearean blank verse, but Marlowe's version was less flexible, with line-ends more clearly marked by both **syntax** and meaning, thus generating an effect of sinewy strength. Within the context of the experimental poetic forms of the 1570s and 1580s it brought a sense of security, confidence and power, while avoiding the jingling effect of **ballad rhythms** or the domination of rhyming.

It is crucial to bear in mind that a play is a performance and not a novel or a series of conversations. Perhaps the hardest thing to spot when reading rather than seeing a play is the effect of placing these fictional words in the mouths of real people. Actors bring their own physical presence to a role and so embody a particular interpretation of that character.

I have not set out to give a complete or dogmatic interpretation of *Edward II* in this Note, but to open up some of the possibilities in the play. You will need to search for further ideas and evidence in the text yourself, and form opinions based on that evidence.

PART TWO

Summaries & Commentaries

The earliest printed edition of Edward II *dates from 1594, the year after Marlowe's death. This contains a title page stating that it had been successfully staged by the Earl of Pembroke's company, and it seems probable that the play was written in 1591. It was one of a cluster of 'history plays' by various authors, based on the Chronicle histories of England and newly fashionable in the early 1590s.* Edward II *was popular both as a play and as a printed book, with further editions in 1598, 1612 and 1622 as well as performances in the 1620s.*

Several good editions of Edward II *are currently available. This Note is based on the New Mermaids edition edited by Martin Wiggins & Robert Lindsey (1997) and follows their division into twenty-five scenes. The Revels Plays version edited by Charles R. Forker (1994) has an extensive Introduction and is very fully annotated, but divides the play anachronistically into acts and scenes.*

Synopsis

One of the earliest of the English history plays to be written, Marlowe's *Edward II* narrates the dramatic and ultimately **tragic** events of the reign of Edward II, based on the Chronicle histories written by **Holinshed** and Stowe. In compressing a long reign of twenty years into a play, Marlowe necessarily selects, organises and makes judgements upon the historical materials he reworks. Many scholars have seen the play as constructed in two 'movements' (to use a term from classical music): the section around Gaveston (Scenes 1–11) and the section around the Spencers (Scenes 11–19). It makes more sense to see it in three 'movements': Edward's loss of Gaveston, his loss of Spencer, and his loss of his own life. This downward structure is counterpointed in the second and third movements against the rise and fall of Mortimer (see Narrative Structure).

The play opens obliquely with Edward's friend Gaveston reading the letter from Edward which recalls him from exile. This has been made possible by Edward's accession to the throne on the death of his father, Edward I. Now able to control his own life, Edward II alienates the nobles around him by his lavish treatment of his favourites. It is not just the considerable expense that is the problem, but also his elevation of people of lowly birth to equal status with the peers. There is thus a dual aspect of economic and social anxiety to the jealous anger of the nobles and churchmen. Edward's brother, Edmund, Earl of Kent (referred to throughout as 'Kent') initially tends to defend Edward's actions. Edward's wife, Queen Isabella, is also distressed by Edward's neglect of her.

The first portion of the play involves a to-and-fro negotiation between the two parties, in which Gaveston is first exiled to Ireland and then recalled. Edward, unreformed, antagonises the nobles yet again, not to mention his brother Kent and his wife Isabella. It seems that the country is becoming poorer very rapidly because of Edward's profligacy and bad management of finances. Civil war ensues. Warwick shows the extremes to which he will go when he ensures that the captured Gaveston is summarily executed without being allowed to say farewell to his friend the King.

With the rift between the two parties becoming more intense, Edward takes a further group of protégés under his wing: the Spencers, father and son, and the shady scholar Baldock. Like Gaveston, none of these is from the nobility, and young Spencer in particular forms a passionately sentimental relationship with Edward. Meanwhile, Edward has won a battle against the nobles, and has Warwick and Lancaster executed together with numerous other opponents.

Mortimer is imprisoned in the Tower, from which Kent soon helps him to escape. In France, these two join forces with Isabella and Edward's son, the young Prince Edward. Mortimer and Isabella embark on an affair. Isabella and Mortimer together with the young Prince and Kent return to England with their army and war against Edward recommences. This time Edward loses the battle and he and his close friends flee for their lives. It may seem that our sympathies should lie with the unhappy Queen Isabella and her son, but it is also clear that Mortimer and Isabella are becoming scheming and vicious. Mortimer in particular behaves tyrannically, and is motivated by a craving for power, not by a desire to govern the country well.

The final movement of the tragedy begins when Edward is captured, hiding amongst the monks at Neath Abbey. His friends Spencer and Baldock are put to death, while Mortimer ensures that Edward himself is placed in increasingly uncomfortable imprisonment. Edward is persuaded to yield the crown to his son, the young Prince Edward, to whom Mortimer will act as Protector until he is old enough to reign. The sadistic murder of Edward by the mysterious Lightborne follows soon after, ending his extreme sufferings in captivity in the dungeon of Berkeley Castle.

The play does not end here, for the 'third movement' has also been concerned with the rise of the unscrupulous Mortimer. The young Prince Edward, now crowned Edward III, has been highly observant and remained loyal to his father throughout, though too young to have any effect on events. Once crowned, however, he rallies support from the nobles to have Mortimer executed for Edward's murder. The play closes with the young King in control, taking part in his father's funeral procession, which is decorated with Mortimer's severed head.

DETAILED SUMMARIES

SCENE 1   **King Edward I has died and the new King Edward II invites his exiled favourite, Gaveston, to return to court, against the advice of his nobles. Tempers flare, and civil war is threatened by the Earl of Warwick, the Mortimers (senior and junior) and the Earl of Lancaster. King Edward defiantly ennobles Gaveston and has the Bishop of Coventry imprisoned**

In an unspecified location, Gaveston is reading a letter from his close friend the King. He expresses his delight in terms that are reminiscent of lovers' meetings. At the same time it is clear that he is not in the least interested in the welfare of the nation, or in helping Edward to govern well. This is further emphasised by his attitude towards the Three Poor Men who now approach him looking for work, for he offers them no rational occupation except to entertain him with lies or to seek charity. In **soliloquy**, Gaveston next imagines a list of frivolous and sensual entertainments for the King, in which he will fill the days and nights with music, dancing and acting.

When the King and nobles arrive, Gaveston hides and watches as the lords try to persuade Edward not to recall his favourite against his dead father's wishes. Edward is determined, and Lancaster's insistence that Gaveston is not noble and so does not deserve Edward's friendship only makes him angry. The conversation quickly escalates into threats on both sides: Mortimer (junior) says that he will no longer fight for the King, Edward threatens Lancaster with violence, and Lancaster suggests that he will raise an army to make war on Edward. Edward's brother, Edmund, Earl of Kent steps in on Edward's side and threatens the nobles with decapitation for daring to oppose the King.

Warwick, Lancaster and the two Mortimers depart angrily to assemble their armies, while Edward and Kent make similar plans. Gaveston now reveals that he has been present all along, and he and Edward greet each other effusively. Edward loads Gaveston with so many titles that even Kent offers a polite objection, only to be roundly silenced by Edward. The Bishop of Coventry enters. He is another who finds Gaveston 'wicked' and who was involved in having him exiled previously. Gaveston and Edward are delighted to take the opportunity to manhandle him, duck him in the gutter and send him to be imprisoned in the Tower. The Bishop's parting words are a curse: 'For this offence be thou accurst of God' (line 198, see Narrative Technique). Again Kent, the voice of reason, tries to restrain Edward, but the scene closes with Edward giving Gaveston the Bishop's house and possessions.

> Much of this obliquely rendered scene reveals Gaveston's character at the same time as it speedily sets out the situation for the audience. It opens with Gaveston reading a letter, a technique which begins the play at a distance from the King himself but using his words. The sexual nature of their relationship is made clear when Gaveston chooses to compare himself with Leander, who swam the Hellespont to meet his lover, Hero. Gaveston here begins a **theme** to do with water which is to recur throughout the play: in this scene alone we find him thinking of a boy 'bathing in a spring'

(line 65), and later the Bishop is ducked in a gutter (see Narrative Technique). In poetic terms resembling the style of the fashionable **epyllion** Gaveston shows his skill at devising lavish entertainments for the King, luxurious recreations that will pander to the King's sensual tendencies and take him away from the business of government. These are mostly theatrical or musical, and it is **ironic** that Marlowe, himself a playwright, should give this rather despicable character a skill similar to his own. Gaveston has few other virtues. His neglect of the Three Poor Men shows both an unChristian and an unpatriotic attitude, as does his remark that he only cares about Edward: 'Not that I love the city or the men, / But that it harbours him I hold so dear' (lines 12–13). The third Poor Man, who has been a soldier and fought for his country, curses Gaveston, and in doing so predicts his death accurately: 'perish by a soldier's hand' (line 36). Gaveston's response suggests that he treats language very lightly, and so is probably not to be trusted. He cares nothing for the Poor Man's curse, and sees his own speech as empty of responsibility when he says 'it is no pain to speak men fair; / I'll flatter these, and make them live in hope' (lines 41–2). The habit of planning ahead makes Gaveston seem especially sinister, as this is a characteristic of the **Morality Play Vice**. When the court enters, he steps aside and functions as an unseen observer and commentator on the nobles: another Vice characteristic. In this way, Gaveston's voice mediates between the action and the audience, and rapidly reveals his own view of these people. The conflict is conducted on a deeply personal level: the lords seem to feel jealous and angry that their noble status does not make them popular with the King.

This scene also shows several characteristic features of Marlowe's **dramaturgy**, in particular the treatment of place and of time. The location must change imperceptibly as the scene proceeds, since from a logical point of view it takes place in several locations:
• Gaveston's place of exile
• the road to London where he meets the Three Poor Men
• the court where the nobles confront Edward
• and lastly the street where the Bishop is assaulted.

3 **surfeit** consume to excess

4 **hap** chance

8 **Leander** in an ancient Greek story, the young man Leander was in love with a beautiful girl called Hero from whom he was separated by a stretch of sea, the Hellespont. To reach her, he regularly swam across the strait, until one night there was a storm and he was drowned

11 **Elysium** the home of the happy dead in ancient Greek mythology

14 **die** Gaveston here plays with the double meaning of the word to form a sexual innuendo

22 *Tanti*! (Italian) 'enough about them'; or 'so many (people)' (a reference to the damned in the first circle of hell in Dante's *Divine Comedy*)

30 **trencher** a container for food, sometimes a simple slab of bread, sometimes a plate

37 **hospital** a charitable residential institution (not a hospital for the sick in the modern sense)

45 **speed well** prosper

54 **Italian masques** lavish plays involving dancing and singing. This is a fashionable entertainment at court in the sixteenth century

57 **sylvan nymphs** spirits of the woods

58 **satyrs** creatures from Greek mythology that are human above the waist and goats below. They were thought to be especially active sexually

59 **antic hay** an old-fashioned peasant dance

60 **Dian** Diana; in ancient mythology, the Goddess of hunting, of the moon and of female chastity

62 **Crownets** coronets

65 **hard by** nearby

66 **Actaeon** another classical story from Ovid. Actaeon the hunter one day chanced to see Diana bathing. In her anger she transformed him into a stag, and his own hounds pursued and killed him

68 **hart** deer

89 *Mort Dieu*! (French) God's death!

110 **Braved** confronted; challenged

117 **Preach upon poles** the decapitated heads would be placed on display on long poles. They then carried a warning to others to avoid treachery, thus 'preaching' **metaphorically**

119 **grant** give in

122 **fence** defend

SCENE 1 continued

125 **parley** negotiate

132 **glozing** flattering; lying

  minion a servant, or a homosexual lover

135 **display my ensigns in the field** raise my flags on the battlefield

136 **bandy** combat

143 **Hylas** an ancient Greek reference to a boy beloved by the mythological champion, Hercules

164 **kingly regiment** ruling as a king, but also (**ambiguously**) conducting oneself in a manner appropriate to a king

167 **seal** token of royal authority

173 **triumphant car** Gaveston refers to the ancient Roman practice of celebrating military victories by bringing prisoners back to Rome, and having them walk beside a chariot in a procession

175 **exequies** funeral. Edward has recalled Gaveston immediately

186 **mitre** Bishop's headdress shaped like a Bishop on a chessboard

  stole priest's garment

187 **channel** gutter

189 **See of Rome** the Pope

195 **use him** treat him

196 **bolts** chains

197 **Tower** the Tower of London, where political and noble prisoners were confined

  the Fleet more down-market prison. The King's remark is dismissive of the Bishop's status

206 **beseem** be appropriate for

SCENE 2 **Warwick, Lancaster and the two Mortimers complain about Edward's behaviour. Isabella is distraught at losing Edward's love, but advises the lords against armed rebellion**

When Warwick and Lancaster chance to meet the Mortimers, it is only natural that they should gossip about the assault on the Bishop in the previous scene. In addition to other honours, Gaveston has now been made Earl of Cornwall, and has taken to swaggering scornfully about the court. Both Lancaster and Mortimer immediately begin to think of violent solutions. When the Bishop of Canterbury enters, angrily sending a messenger to the Pope about the Bishop of Coventry's maltreatment, the nobles immediately invite him to join a rebellion against the King. Mortimer modifies this to a proposal that Gaveston be either banished or beheaded. At this point, Queen Isabella enters, leaving court for a quieter life since she cannot bear to be so neglected by her husband. Mortimer, Lancaster and Warwick ask her to participate in a rebellion to remove Gaveston, but neither she nor the Bishop are in favour of such hostilities. She loves him too much to make him unhappy. The Bishop considers it immoral to depose a King. The Bishop then suggests that the King's council could officially banish Gaveston, and this plan is agreed.

> This short scene moves the plot forward by collecting together those who have reason to feel discomfited by Edward and Gaveston. The lords are offended that a man of humble origins whom they describe as 'villain' (line 11) and 'peasant' (line 30) has become Earl of Cornwall, and officially their equal. He is also an outsider because he is foreign: they call him a 'sly, inveigling Frenchman' (line 57), not noticing that Isabella is also French. The Bishop of Canterbury is angry both about the offence done to the Church and about the loss of Church possessions. Isabella though distressed is willing to live away from the court if that will make Edward happy. Some editors read her plans to go to 'the forest' as a **metaphor** for her sense of alienation, but there seems no reason to suppose that she does not also mean it literally. Isabella's advice against armed rebellion seems reasonable, and characterises her as both virtuous and victimised, though in closing she addresses Mortimer as 'sweet Mortimer' (line 81), perhaps implying the beginning of their affection.

6 **sepulchre** tomb
11 **villain** peasant, but also capable of meaning an evil person
16 **post** hurry
   levy men raise an army
19 **vailing of his bonnet** raising his hat
26 **stomach** feel ill at putting up with (Gaveston)
27 **bewrays** displays
29 **hale** haul, pull

37 **asseized** confiscated by the Crown

38 **This certify the Pope** swear to the truth of this to the Pope

57 **inveigling** sneaking into favour

75 **New Temple** a building belonging to the Knights Templar

78 **Lambeth** Lambeth Palace is the residence of the Archbishop of Canterbury

82 **Forbear to** refrain from

SCENE 3   **Gaveston tells Kent that the nobles have gone to Lambeth**

Gaveston lists the group of nobles who have met at Lambeth, showing his contempt for them. Those involved are Lancaster, Warwick and the two Mortimers. Gaveston is unconcerned about the collusion. Kent, accompanying Gaveston, says nothing.

> It is clear that news travels fast in London, for Gaveston is immediately aware that the nobles have gathered. He denigrates Lancaster by associating the idea of his titles with an ass, a term which can also mean 'idiot'. The others he praises in sarcastic terms. The presence of Kent may seem puzzling. It has the effect of showing that Kent is still on his brother's side, but his failure to speak could be used in performance to show growing dissatisfaction with Gaveston's scorn for the values of the nobility. This short scene, intervening between two conversations amongst the rebellious nobles, maintains a rhythm whereby scenes move alternately between the nobles and the courtly group they wish to demolish. The effect is to increase the pace of the play by keeping the audience in touch with developments on both sides.

4 **redoubted** famous

SCENE 4   **A confrontation takes place at court and Gaveston is exiled. Edward blames Isabella, refusing to see her unless she can have Gaveston recalled. Isabella persuades Mortimer to influence the nobles. He succeeds by suggesting that Gaveston might be more easily murdered in London. The King, mourning for Gaveston's departure, is delighted to hear that he is allowed to return, and treats both Isabella and the nobles more warmly. Gaveston is to marry Edward's niece, Lady Margaret. Mortimer senior departs for the Scottish wars**

The lords eagerly sign a warrant for Gaveston to be exiled again. At court, they find that Gaveston now occupies a throne next to Edward, effectively giving him at least the Queen's proper status, and perhaps even near-equality with the King. The scene begins violently, with an armed confrontation between the nobles and Edward, in which Gaveston and Kent are seized by the well-armed nobles through sheer force of numbers and greater preparedness for aggressive behaviour. Edward attempts to resist their decisiveness, but soon sees that he will be involved in civil war or even deposed through the authority of the Bishop if he persists. Apparently in order to preserve his reign, Edward offers to divide the administration of the kingdom among the nobles, keeping only a small area where he and Gaveston could live. The lords treat this suggestion as empty **rhetoric**, and insist on full banishment to which Edward sorrowfully accedes.

Blaming Isabella, Edward refuses to see her until Gaveston can return. This motivates Isabella powerfully with desperate emotions. Seeing that she will be miserable whether Gaveston is at court or not, Isabella sets out to persuade the nobles to allow Gaveston to return. Mortimer is converted by her persuasions, but the audience does not know what she said, as she speaks to him separately. Mortimer in turn persuades the nobles, by pointing out that Gaveston could raise a rebellion while he is exiled in Ireland. It would be safer, therefore, to keep him at court where he can be watched, and where the nobles can have him murdered. 'How easily might some base slave be suborned / To greet his lordship with a poniard' (lines 265–6). Mortimer also hopes that being sent to and fro like this will show Gaveston how much power the lords have over him, and so humble him. "Twill make him vail the topflag of his pride' (line 276). If this does not work, the nobles will feel that they have a good excuse for rebellion, because the people will join with them against the offensive Gaveston. 'So shall we have the people of our side' (line 282).

The scene draws to a close with the nobles all given honours and functions within the government, and wedding plans being made for Gaveston and Lady Margaret, the King's 'cousin' (relative). Lastly, Mortimer senior leaves for Scotland, advising Mortimer to be patient. Mortimer's response is not promising.

> In this volatile and exciting scene the various motives of those who are opposed to Gaveston become more clearly defined. The Mortimers are especially offended by Gaveston's low social origins, persistently describing him in insulting terms such as 'base peasant' (line 7). The sight of Gaveston seated on an equal footing with the King enrages all the lords. Edward believes that his word must be obeyed, while the nobles believe that the King has a duty to preserve the hierarchy of the state. Thus by each group's lights, the other is clearly in the wrong. A conflict between two versions of the moral high ground is unlikely to be easily resolved. Edward makes a fascinating offer: to retire from government, leaving power divided amongst the nobles, and live privately with Gaveston. The Elizabethan period was notoriously uneasy about the idea of a divided realm (Shakespeare's *King Lear* showed disasters ensuing from just such a division), and Marlowe shows Edward's suggestion instantly brushed aside by the Bishop of Canterbury. Edward, significantly, says that he is 'content' (line 85) to sign because 'I see I must' (line 85): two words with powerful loadings for the drama. Clearly, he is far from 'content' with the arrangement, but uses this word, often used deceitfully on the Elizabethan stage, to mean that he is willing. The word alone flags up Edward's potential for repudiating his word of honour, as embodied in his signature. 'Must' too is a word that will reappear later with great weight, as Edward believes that a king should not be instructed to do anything. The central portion of the scene involves a triple persuasion: first Edward blackmails Isabella into helping him, then

Isabella enlists Mortimer's help and lastly Mortimer manages to change the lords' minds about the best course of action. It is revelational to see how these different persuasions work. Edward effectively coerces Isabella, threatening her with his anger, and with the withdrawal of affection if she does not have Gaveston recalled. Quite unjustly, he believes her to be responsible for the exile.

At her most poignant moment, Isabella realises that she cannot be happy with Edward whether Gaveston is present or absent, and so chooses to sacrifice her own happiness to her husband's desires by working to have Gaveston recalled. The conversation which she then conducts with Mortimer is tantalisingly inaudible, and scholars have suggested that she is flirting with Mortimer at this early stage of the relationship. There is no evidence for or against this, but it makes a difference to how one reads Isabella's character. If one believes her to be immediately flirtatious with Mortimer, having decided to cut her losses and opt for a comfortable affair, this makes her especially calculating and fickle. If one sees her more generously, then we assume that the arguments uttered privately are the same as those offered by Mortimer to the nobles, and we simply do not hear them from Isabella as they are dramatically more effective coming from Mortimer. Mortimer puts three separate arguments to the other nobles, all to do with a pragmatic approach to politics, and therefore **Machiavellian** in tone. They are:

- Gaveston might raise an army while in Ireland, and return to overthrow them by force.
- Recalling him would make it possible to employ a local murderer. Mortimer's own attitude to this is oddly contradictory, for he describes this murderer contemptuously as 'some base slave', but also describes the murder itself as something honourable, that would cause the murderer to be praised, and remembered in history.
- Gaveston will in future be humbler.
- If he is not, that will give them an excuse to rise in rebellion. In that circumstance, Mortimer believes that the common people would join them.

Clearly, then, the lords are persuaded to recall Gaveston by a series of arguments that offer them what they really want: his extinction. Reconciliation seems almost impossible, yet at this point in the scene it is attempted, and soon shown to be too fragile to last. All goes according to plan: Gaveston is recalled, Isabella forgiven and the lords pleased to be in Edward's good graces again. The reconciliation scene shows all the main characters on a new footing, all with hopes and expectations, but in the case of the nobles also with pragmatic plans for taking alternative actions should the peace fail. The apparent content of the section in which wedding plans are made and the nobles treated kindly is undermined by the threatening tone of the dialogue that follows between the two Mortimers. The older Mortimer counsels patience and tolerance, but Mortimer continues angry, not only at the financial excesses, but also over the style in which money is wasted. He characterises the latter as

- monstrous ('outlandish cullions' line 410, 'fantastic liveries' line 411)
- foreign ('short Italian hooded cloak' line 414, 'Tuscan cap' line 415)
- transgressive of class boundaries (line 404), and
- insolent (lines 417–419).

2 **subscribe your name** sign your name

7 **declined** turned away from

8 **moved** angry

12 **brook** tolerate

13 *Quam male conveniunt*! (Latin) What a mismatched couple! Ovid, *Metamorphoses*, II.846–7 (Wiggins & Lindsey)

16 **Phaëthon** a character from ancient Greek mythology, who in his pride and ambition believed he could drive the chariot that pulls the sun. He was unable to control the horses, caused drought and fires on earth and crashed to his death. Ovid *Metamorphoses* I.755ff

19 **faced** challenged, confronted

over-peered an invented word which combines the senses of being looked down on and having a noble (peer) set up above them

26 **pay them home** even the score

49 **fleet** float away

50 **Inde** the Indies

51 **legate to the Pope** ambassador from the Pope

59 **abused** assaulted

61 **discharge these lords** free these lords from their duty

63 **It boots me not** it does me no good

68 **President** governor, viceroy

82 **lown** coarse person, peasant

89 **published** read out in public

90 **presently dispatched** sent off immediately

100 **crazèd** cracked, broken

102 **Tiber** river in Rome

132 **grieve** injure, pain

142 **I pass not** I don't care

172 **Circe** a sorceress in Homer's *Odyssey* and in Ovid's *Metamorphoses*, who turned Odysseus's men into swine

174 **Hymen** ancient Greek and Roman god of marriage

178, 180 **frantic Juno** in classical myth, Juno was a goddess and the wife of **Jove**. She became desperately jealous when Jove fancied the cup-bearer, **Ganymede**, a beautiful boy

189 **entreated** spoken to

191 **long of** because of

211 **as thou lovest and tend'rest** if you are loyal to me and value me. Isabella is not necessarily speaking romantically

223 **torpedo** sting-ray

237 **grant** agree

243 **behoof** benefit

250 **what he can allege** what arguments he can put forward

255 **play the sophister** put forward arguments which seem to prove something without actually doing so, after the Sophists, a group of philosophers of ancient Greece

257 **mend** amend, improve

260 **front** attack

265 **suborned** bribed

266 **poniard** short sword, dagger

269 **chronicle** history (see Literary Background)

276 **vail the topflag** lower the highest flag on a ship (a signal of submission in battle)

279 **colour** excuse

280 **howsoever we have borne it out** however we have represented it

281 **to be up against the King** to raise an army against the King

284 **a night-grown mushroom** an upstart (i.e. Gaveston). The whole sentence means: 'In this way, the people, who naturally favour the King, because they liked his father, will come over to our side, because they cannot bear to see the nobility pushed aside by an upstart like the Earl of Cornwall (i.e. Gaveston)'

288 **buckler** protect (a buckler was a shield)

314 **Cyclops** a race of one-eyed giant blacksmiths in ancient Greek myth. Their task was to hammer out thunderbolts for Zeus

317 **Fury** the Erinyes or Furies in ancient Greece were a trio of mythological female demons from the Underworld who tormented wrongdoers

320 **Diablo**! (Spanish) = the devil!

322 **parlied** spoken, negotiated, but with an additional possible sense of 'had sex with'. Edward again is suspicious of his wife's honour

354 **aside** alone, separate from the others

372 **Iris** mythological character representing the rainbow; she could function as a messenger
Jove's Mercury character from Roman mythology. Mercury (Hermes in Greek) was always represented with winged sandals, to show that he is the messenger of the Gods

385 **aught** anything

393 **Alexander** Alexander the Great, a Macedonian Emperor
Hephaestion a general in Alexander's army, with whom he had a close friendship

394 **Hercules for Hylas wept** the hero, Hercules, felt tenderly towards the boy Hylas, who was swept overboard and drowned

395 **for Patroclus stern Achilles drooped** in the *Iliad*, the Greek hero Achilles mourns the death of his intimate friend Patroclus

397 **Tully loved Octavius** Tully is another name for the orator Cicero, whose writings were especially highly venerated in the Renaissance

398 **Socrates, wild Alcibiades** Socrates is the ancient Greek philosopher, and Alcibiades one of his close friends and pupils

409 **Midas-like** in the legend everything that King Midas touched turned to gold. Thus, Gaveston is wearing huge quantities of gold and gold cloth at court

jets it walks proudly up and down

410 **cullions** oafs, low servants

412 **Proteus** in mythology a shape-shifting sea god

413 **dapper jack** fashionably dressed upstart

413 **brisk** smartly turned-out

419 **flout our train** utter provocative, sneering remarks at our companions

SCENE 5   **Spencer and Baldock resolve to join Gaveston. Lady Margaret, Gaveston's fiancée, plans to go to court to meet Gaveston. The three depart together**

The Earl of Gloucester, the lord served by Spencer junior and Baldock, has recently died. Spencer resolves to try to make his way in the world by befriending Gaveston (referred to here as Earl of Cornwall). Gloucester's daughter Lady Margaret has a long-standing affection for Gaveston. Baldock has the humble subservient appearance of a stereotypical scholar, but Spencer recommends that he become a courtier. Baldock takes to this suggestion, including the violence and deception that he believes to be a part of that lifestyle. Lady Margaret enters, reading a letter from Gaveston, and then a letter from the King, inviting her to court immediately.

> This scene introduces new characters. There is a considerable relief for the audience at moving away from the mental anguish of Edward's court at this point, and from a dramatic point of view it is a good moment to allow for some presumed passage of time. Spencer and Baldock are friends, though of slightly different stations in life (see Themes, on England). Spencer has been a gentleman-servant and Baldock a tutor to Lady Margaret. This places Spencer higher up the social scale than the employee Baldock, though both are dependent for their livelihood on the goodwill of the person for whom they work. (At line 71 it is Baldock who is curtly sent to see that Lady Margaret's coach is made ready, while Spencer is her confidant.) Baldock explains that his previous respectable appearance was entirely deceitful. In terms reminiscent of the stage **Vice** or **Machiavel**, he describes his

hypocrisy, and his willingness to indulge in various kinds of corruption. This is a little puzzling for the audience, for Vice characteristics traditionally tell us whose side we should be on, and whom we should be against. In this play, however, Mortimer appears to make plots and schemes just as Baldock does: untrustworthy cynicism appears on both sides of the debate. The sympathy we may feel for each side is moderated by their follies, and few are unequivocally virtuous. When Lady Margaret enters, she does not notice Spencer or Baldock at first: they may have stepped to the side or rear of the stage, a spy-like move which makes them seem well-suited to the intrigues and eavesdroppings of the court.

14 **preferred (ambiguous)** Spencer may mean that Gaveston recommended him to the King, or he may mean that Gaveston liked him better than he liked the King. The former meaning is more likely

35 **nosegay** a little bunch of sweet-smelling flowers, used to help ward off rank smells

37 **table's end** the foot of the table. Seating at the table indicated status: the lord at the head and the humblest person at the foot

49 **curate-like** dressed very plainly, like a junior clergyman

53 ***propterea quod*** (Latin) because of that

54 ***quandoquidem*** (Latin) because of that

67 **repair** move

73 **park pale** the fence which marks the edge of the Earl's property, or park

presently immediately

SCENE 6   **At Tynemouth where they have gathered to welcome Gaveston back from Ireland, the uneasy truce between Edward and the lords becomes more fragile. Tempers are short and insults exchanged, Gaveston is wounded. Civil war becomes a likelihood. Next Edward refuses to ransom the captive Mortimer senior, angering the lords and alienating his brother Kent. Baldock and Spencer are introduced to Edward, and the marriage between Gaveston and the Lady Margaret is imminent**

Mortimer tries to make Edward focus on the business of government, but the latter is obsessed with Gaveston. The King of France has attacked Normandy, but Edward wishes to plan the pageant that will welcome Gaveston. Mortimer and Lancaster, asked to describe the **emblems** they will use, tactlessly display their distaste for Gaveston. When Gaveston disembarks, he is joyfully greeted by the King, and mockingly greeted by his various titles by the lords. The conversation quickly deteriorates into an exchange of abuse, which ends in Mortimer wounding Gaveston with a sword. Edward bans Mortimer from the court as a punishment, threatening the other lords with execution when they protest. Kent sides with Edward, and the lords withdraw to their castles to collect their armies in order to dispose of Gaveston by force. At that moment letters arrive from Scotland, announcing the capture of Mortimer's uncle. The ransom demanded is so large that only the King could possibly pay it. Furthermore, Mortimer senior was captured while leading an army on behalf of the King, so Edward has a moral obligation to ransom him. Edward instead insults the lords by giving them permission to beg to collect the ransom. Enraged, they confront Edward with a detailed description of his shortcomings as a monarch and a general, and storm out. Seeing his brother's intransigence, Kent now fears civil war and joins the nobles. Edward reacts by longing for solitude, and then unjustly accusing Isabella of causing the conflict. He and Gaveston consider employing a murderer to do away with Mortimer. At this point they notice Baldock and Spencer, who introduce themselves and are immediately accepted as friends. The scene ends with a plan for Gaveston's wedding to Lady Margaret.

> In a scene of enormous emotional variety, joy, sarcasm, anger and violence are all experienced in turn. The emblems need explanation. Gaveston is a 'canker' or decay that attacks Edward (represented as a cedar). The motto 'equal at last' suggests quite explicitly that Gaveston has long sought to be the social equal of the peers (the eagles). Lancaster's emblem of a flying fish refers to a creature that moves outside its natural element (as Gaveston has moved outside his proper sphere). Lancaster threatens that it will die wherever it goes. This strange creature is an example of the unnatural (see Historical Background, on Nature/the Unnatural) a theme which runs through the play. Edward reads the language of

the pictures accurately, and is understandably furious with the lords.
Neither party is willing to make any compromise for the sake of a
peaceful future. The extent of the lovers' feeling is imaged in the
elaborate language they use: Edward compares himself to a lover of
Danaë, Gaveston sees himself as a joyful shepherd. This is a
relationship that takes place at least in part on an imaginative and
literary level, which pictures itself in **metaphor**, rather than in
literal terms. Indeed, the clash with the lords might be said to be a
competition over the metaphoric construction of the lovers, for we
have heard them describing Gaveston in aggressive and damaging
terms as a 'canker' (line 18), just before he identifies with pastoral,
mordant imagery of victimisation 'the shepherd nipped with biting
winter's rage' (line 60). The anger that swiftly follows bubbles over
uncontrollably: Marlowe is a master at representing how hasty
speech leads people to say things they regret, and also to utter
things that they have previously merely thought. Either way, this
kind of escalating row moves the plot rapidly towards violence.
There is a childish element about the irascibility of both groups. It
also leaves them open to manipulation by cooler minds such as
Mortimer's. Mortimer takes advantage of the atmosphere to
attempt to murder Gaveston, but only wounds him.

There is no evidence in the text that this attack is calculated,
but one could perform it in that way to represent Mortimer as a
plotter rather than as impulsive. It is hardly surprising in these
circumstances that Edward now refuses their request for money
to ransom Mortimer senior, taken prisoner in Scotland, even
though, rationally, he ought to accede. This financial issue focuses
the lords' complaints that too much is spent on Gaveston and on
pleasure, as it has left the King with insufficient funds to perform
his duty by his subjects. It springboards Lancaster and Mortimer
into the shared tirade of abuse in which they ritualistically surround
Edward with a barrage of complaints and criticisms: he neglects his
wife, the border areas are under attack and Edward himself is an
incompetent soldier and a laughing-stock. Kent sees the ruinous
course that his brother is on, and feels that the whole situation
would be solved if Gaveston were banished. Edward is under-

standably furious and, in the first of his changes of heart, Kent leaves to join the nobles, clearly hurt that Edward has dismissed his advice.

Bizarrely, Edward now comforts Gaveston and seems oblivious to the damage he has done to his own position as king. His imaginary solitude with Gaveston is completely impractical, but the concept reveals his mental state: he relishes the drama of the situation in which he and his lover are isolated in a simple location, surrounded by enemies. It is strikingly effective that at this instant Gaveston enters, but not alone. He is accompanied by Isabella making an unwelcome third and what must feel like a crowd of Edward's supporters: Lady Margaret with two other ladies, Baldock and Spencer. Edward turns on the Queen, accusing her of complicity with Mortimer, but is surreptitiously advised to retract by Gaveston. Once again, the King is involved in the plots and deceit that would normally be ascribed to an evil character. In this way our reaction to him is made equivocal, and our sympathies lie more strongly with Isabella. This is intensified when we find that Gaveston and Edward are laying plans to murder Mortimer. This exchange should take place **aside**, ending halfway through line 236 at 'but let them go', and moving to public utterance when Edward addresses Lady Margaret with 'and tell me what are these?' (line 236).

The **theme** of social class returns in Baldock's self-description 'my gentry / I fetched from Oxford, not from heraldry' (lines 240–1). In other words, he has graduated from university which means that he could be considered a gentleman, but he has no family connections amongst the gentry. Edward's response suggests that a lowly born person might be useful. 'The fitter art thou Baldock, for my turn' (line 242). His 'turn' could in theory be anything useful, but it carries both a sexual and a sinister undercurrent. In the context of the earlier plot, it sounds as if he means to pay Baldock to commit murder, while in the context of Edward's proclivities it could also imply that Baldock will be made subordinate in the sexual games. Spencer receives a very different welcome because Gaveston knows him personally and because he is related to a noble family. Edward promises him a title. The third of

Edward's offers in this gift-giving scene is of his niece Lady
Margaret as a wife to Gaveston, thus effectively making Gaveston a
member of the royal family.

9 **sets foot in** has invaded
11 **device** an invented design painted on the shield of a participant in a
tournament. Such a design would usually have some significance which was
flattering to the monarch or to the principal guest
12 **Against** prepared for; ready for
triumph celebration involving costumes, parades and games
20 ***Æque tandem*** (Latin) equal at last. Gaveston has climbed up to the same
height as the nobles, and in doing so has destroyed the King, who supports
all of them
23 **Pliny** Latin writer who wrote the *Natural History*, in which he described
many animals both real and mythological
28 ***Undique mors est*** (Latin) death is everywhere. In theory, this motto is
unobjectionable popular theology, but, when it is associated with the flying
fish (Gaveston) which has risen out of its element, the words become a
threat
40 **jesses** leather straps by which birds of prey could be controlled
46 **harpy** mythological creature, part bird and part woman, which attacks
human beings
47 **whenas** when
51 **Tynemouth** a seaport in the north-east of England, at the mouth of the River
Tyne, near Newcastle. Edward is thus a long way from London, and
vulnerably close to traditionally rebellious areas
53 **Danaë** in ancient Greek mythology, this beautiful young woman was locked
up by her father. The God Zeus found his way to her by changing himself
into a shower of gold
72 **jar** argue
87 **aby** pay for
109 ***Enter a*** POST *enter a messenger*
121 **gather head** collect an army
123 **I warrant you** I promise
129 **marry** indeed (the short form of an oath on the Virgin Mary)
134 **You may not in** you are not allowed to go in (to the King)
136 **How now** what's this? (a common exclamation)

144–5 **the broad seal / To gather for him** official permission to collect money on his behalf

161 **kerns** ordinary soldiers; peasants

162 **pale** a protected settlement made by the colonising English in Ireland

180 **players** actors

184 **women's favours** small items of apparel such as scarves or gloves, given to the lady's favourite knight in a tournament or battle

185 **fleering** scornful, jeering

186 **jig** short ballad, often crude or offensive

188 **lemans** lovers

Bannockburn a battle between the English and the Scots in which the English lost decisively (1314)

190 **weeneth** thinks, expects

192 **rumbelow** nonsense word used as a refrain

193 **Wigmore shall fly** he will sell his family estate of Wigmore Castle

198 **baited** tormented (as in bear-baiting)

220 **begirt us round** surround us

221 **jars** quarrels; discord

226 **dissemble** hide your true thoughts

233 **privily made away** secretly murdered

234 **caroused** taken a celebratory drink; toasted

238 **entertain them** permit them to serve you

240–1 **my gentry / I fetched from Oxford** I am a gentleman because I graduated from Oxford University

242 **fitter** more appropriate

243 **Wait on me** be my servant

250 **style** title

260 **list** wish

262 **complices** accomplices; companions

SCENE 7   **Kent arrives at the rebel camp near Tynemouth Castle.
At first Lancaster and Warwick are suspicious of his
sincerity, but soon take his word. They attack the castle**

Arriving at the camp, Kent explains that he is joining them because he cares about his country's condition. He is not readily believed, and Lancaster suspects that he is secretly there to subvert the lords, while

Warwick thinks that family loyalty to his brother renders his arrival suspicious. Mortimer, however, is prepared to accept Kent's word of honour as a Plantagenet. Lancaster now (perhaps unnecessarily) informs the others that the King and Gaveston are revelling in the castle together, and a sudden attack would defeat them. The attack begins with the sound of drums and Lancaster's reminder not to hurt the King.

> Nobility continues to be a **theme** in this scene, as it is Kent's descent from the royal Plantagenet family that motivates Mortimer to trust him. This reliance on family honour is a feudal characteristic, coherent with Mortimer's wish to carry his ancestor's banner into battle (lines 21–2) and his reference to the origins of the family name (lines 22–3). Both Mortimer and Kent explicitly refer to their francophone origins in this scene as a source of their nobility, which is puzzling in the light of their claim that England is their 'native land' (line 1) and their condemnation of Gaveston as foreign (see Themes, on England). Traditionally, secrecy is associated with 'policy' and with the less-than-noble classes. Thus, it is especially insulting to accuse Kent of 'policy' (line 5), as that would align him with the likes of Gaveston, who has arrived 'secretly' (line 16), or of Baldock whom Edward plans to use in as-yet-unspecified but clearly ignoble ways (see Scene 6, line 242). This is **paradoxical** in Mortimer, who himself appears to be quite willing to plot in secret, to be treacherous towards his King, and to plan the murder of Gaveston – all highly ignoble activities. Yet at the same time, he values nobility highly. Mortimer is thus contradictory and even deeply hypocritical. Alternatively, one might see him as unable to perceive his own actions in their true light. If Mortimer's character is consistent throughout, then one might take the former attitude, while the latter fits with a theory that he changes as the action proceeds (as does Isabella). The co-operation amongst the rebels is imaged in the tightly structured three-way conversation and the ease with which plans are made and carried out. It is Lancaster who moves the conversation on from Kent's *bona fides* to a suggestion that they attack the castle. Mortimer immediately agrees to start the attack, and Warwick to follow him. Thus tactics are amicably and spontaneously arranged.

Lancaster's reminder not to harm the King sounds a note of common-sense in their headlong rush.

3 **the realm's behoof** for the kingdom's sake

5 **policy** cunning: a feature of the **Machiavellian** attitude to politics

6 **a show of love** a pretence of allegiance

8 **cast** forecast; speculate

25 **alarum** to arms! the signal to attack

SCENE **8**   **Edward loses the battle. He and Gaveston are pursued and Isabella leaves for France**

The battle is going badly. Edward and Gaveston separate and flee, Gaveston by ship to Scarborough, Edward on horseback over land. Isabella, alone, expresses her continued love for Edward, contrary to his reiterated opinion that she is having an affair with Mortimer. When Lancaster, Mortimer and Warwick enter in hot pursuit of Gaveston, they are sympathetic towards her distress and suggest that she should accompany them. She, however, plans to follow Edward and tells them how to find Gaveston. They hasten after him. Alone again, Isabella muses in **soliloquy** on Mortimer's virtues, and, changing her mind about following her rejecting husband, makes plans to leave England for France, where she can enlist the help of her brother, the King of France.

Many critics have found Isabella's change of heart puzzling. In this scene, her motivations are made clear, as we see her going through a range of connected emotions. First, sorrow and loneliness, and a sense of being misjudged. Edward, believing her to be in league with the lords, leaves her behind when the castle is overrun, while he saves himself and Gaveston. Next she expresses despair of ever succeeding in getting Edward back as long as Gaveston is alive. She does not realise that Edward's dislike of her is to do with his own sexuality, but blames it entirely on Gaveston, enabling her to live in hope. While this excuses Edward and enables her to see him as a victim of Gaveston's wiles, it is unrealistic. At the crisis of the battle, she realises how intransigent Edward is towards her, and how fixed is his belief in her infidelity. His farewells to all but Isabella show how profoundly he has rejected her: he no longer includes her in even the ordinary human rituals of greeting and

SCENE 8 continued

farewell. His suspicion affects her capacity even to speak with the only people who are pleasant to her. At line 36 she takes the crucial decision to betray Gaveston to the lords who seek his death. In this decision she can still hold to her theory that Gaveston's death will restore Edward to her, while at the same time helping Mortimer. This moment when she is not fully committed to either side might be seen as transitional in Isabella's emotions as she holds contradictory opinions simultaneously. She now has a plan in case Edward rejects her again. Her decision to leave for her home country is still a temporising step, by which she hopes that her brother might influence matters for the better. It is not clear how he could, nor is it clear what kind of outcome she now perceives as feasible.

Unlike Edward, Mortimer finds time in the middle of the pursuit to attempt to look after Isabella and to ensure that she has plans. When the scene closes, she has Mortimer in mind as well as Edward, and a much more purposeful set of plans than she had at the beginning of the scene. This is an emotionally subtle scene, exploring how Isabella's mind continues to function and her emotions to progress even when under extremes of pressure.

5 **Scarborough** a seaport at the mouth of the Tyne River

27 **haling** pulling

40 **his train is small** there are few people with him

41 **Forslow no time** hurry up

47 **hoy** small fishing vessel

48 **amain** quickly

57 **gentle** noble

65 **strange** distant and uncaring

SCENE 9   **Gaveston is captured. A message from Edward pleads to see him one last time. Escorted by the Earl of Pembroke, Gaveston travels to say farewell to Edward**

Gaveston enters, fleeing and hoping to escape capture. Within moments he is overtaken by the angry nobles, who order his execution. Gaveston accepts his fate, but they are interrupted by a messenger (Lord Maltravers, Earl of Arundel) bringing the King's plea to speak to

Gaveston and say good-bye before the latter is executed. The lords, suspicious of Edward's good faith, respond brutally and insultingly, calling Gaveston a 'thief' (line 70) and a 'base groom' (line 72). The Earl of Pembroke relents, and offers to guarantee that Gaveston will be returned to be executed after a last meeting. Against Warwick's judgement, the nobles agree to let Gaveston travel under armed guard to see Edward. Pembroke chooses to overnight *en route* at his own castle of Cobham, leaving Gaveston in the charge of James and a small group of other men.

In another fast-moving scene, reminiscent of the style of cinema chases, we begin by seeing the pursuit from Gaveston's point of view. Time is compressed in a surreal way, as the flight, the capture, the news of the capture reaching the King, and the appearance of a messenger from Edward all occur within seconds of one another on stage. Significantly more time is spent on the argument over the King's request and whether it might be trusted. The King wishes to see Gaveston one last time, and promises to send him back to his death afterwards. In disbelieving him, the lords cast a slur on Edward's honour. Edward will 'Violate any promise to possess him [Gaveston]' (line 64) says Warwick. Maltravers then honourably offers to act as Gaveston's 'pledge' (line 66) – that is, he will be a hostage, and if Gaveston does not return, Maltravers will be executed in his stead. Mortimer's answer insults Gaveston by implying that the substitution would not be a fair one: he will not execute a man of honour as a substitute for a criminal. Gaveston objects to this insult, demanding to know what Mortimer means (though he understands perfectly well) and describing the insult as 'over-base' (line 71). This may mean that it is beneath Mortimer to say such a thing, or Mortimer has called Gaveston by too lowly a description. Mortimer re-emphasises his insult by asserting that he sees Gaveston as a thief of the King's reputation. He explains that he is so much superior to Gaveston that he need not speak to him directly: Gaveston should speak to his own (lowly) social equals ('thy companions and the mates', line 73).

Pembroke persuades the other lords that he can take Gaveston to the King and back reliably, but Warwick like a stage villain plots to

SCENE 9 continued

assassinate Gaveston on the way. The opportunity for Warwick to cause mischief will arise when Pembroke stays overnight with his wife at Cobham. Here again we find the geographical awareness that informs much of this play: even a minor character like Pembroke is shown to have a home in an identifiable location (see Themes, on England). That the pursuit should now be near Cobham in the south-east suggests that sufficient time must have passed to allow for the passage by sea from Scarborough in the north-east.

- *1* **lusty** energetic; strong-willed
- *2* **'larums** short for 'alarums': sounding the charge into battle
- *5* **malgrado all your beards** in spite of your attempts
- *15* **the Greekish strumpet** Helen of Troy
- *18* **buckler** protect (as with a shield)
- *30* **heading** execution by beheading
- *60* **we wot** we know
- *62* **exigents** exigencies; extremes
- *93* **how 'twill prove** how things will turn out
- *96* **wit and policy** intelligence and cunning
- *98* **Sound away!** Mortimer instructs the trumpeter to sound the signal for departure
- *103* **balk** deny; disappoint
- *105* **adamant** magnet (Maltravers is making a compliment to Pembroke's wife, saying that she has the power of a magnet, in that she can attract him (Pembroke) who is a Prince)
- *111* **Cobham** Pembroke's home: thought to be the village in Kent rather than the one in Surrey. Cobham is relatively close to the Thames, and so would be convenient for people travelling by sea to London

SCENE 10   Gaveston is captured by Warwick and his soldiers, and taken offstage to his death

The unarmed Gaveston with James and the servants are under attack. They realise that it is Warwick who has followed them with his superior forces. Gaveston tells the servants to hurry to inform the King. Warwick takes Gaveston off to execution, leaving James to report events.

Warwick is convinced that he is doing the best thing for his country in executing Gaveston, and so does not consider his actions to be dishonourable. It is courageous of the servant James to challenge him, and it shows Warwick's respect for Pembroke that he is prepared to give James (Pembroke's servant) a rational answer. In Warwick's mouth, this play's characteristic 'Away!' (line 17) displays his dominance but also the speed and panache with which he functions and keeps events moving forward. 'Away' here is extra-metrical, that is, it does not belong rhythmically with the lines before or after it, which makes the word especially prominent. Many actors would leave a space of four beats, as if to fill up the **iambic pentameter** line, before speaking the next line.

3 **in bands** in bonds; tied up
4 **period** conclusion
5 **An ye be** if you are
7 **strive** fight
14 **shadow** departed spirit; ghost
    parley converse
18 **it booted not for us to strive** it would have been no good to fight
19 **certify** tell with certainty; vow

SCENE 11   **Incited by Spencer, Edward determines to use force against the rebel lords. Queen Isabella and Prince Edward leave for France to enlist the King of France's support. Maltravers brings news of Gaveston's death. Edward, vowing revenge, elevates Spencer to Gaveston's place. A messenger from the lords offers peace if Edward will send Spencer away. Edward responds by threatening war**

Edward is as yet unaware of Gaveston's death, but realises that it is inevitable. Young Spencer, reminding Edward of his noble lineage, encourages him to plan to force the lords to release Gaveston. Spencer's father (old Spencer) enters and offers soldiers to support Edward, who gives them generous sums of money. At this point Queen Isabella arrives with Prince Edward, carrying out her plan (from Scene 8) to make one last attempt at reconciliation with her husband. Edward decides that Isabella and their son should travel to France to negotiate with the King

(Isabella's brother) and gain his support against the lords. They depart, and Maltravers arrives with news of Gaveston's death. Edward is furiously angry, and threatens bloody retribution. He gives Gaveston's titles to Spencer, and immediately a messenger arrives from the lords demanding that he send Spencer away. The cycle seems set to repeat itself as Edward collects an army to impose his authority on the lords.

This scene towards the centre of the play sees a transition from the first phase, the loss of Gaveston, into the second phase, the loss of Spencer. With **dramatic irony** Edward is unaware that Gaveston is already dead and makes plans to save him. These include collecting support from various unlikely sources: the aged father of Spencer and the foreign King of France (to whom he already owes money). His support therefore comes from the periphery of his kingdom: from people who are marginal to Englishness, to masculinity and to power (see Themes, on England). Dismissing his debt to the King of France as trivial, Edward shows his poor judgement and lack of diplomatic skill. He asks his young son (another peripheral and powerless figure) to act as a messenger to the King of France. Prince Edward displays wisdom in pointing out that he is too young for the task, and courage in promising to do his best and keep his father's trust. At this, Isabella utters an **aphorism** to the effect that those who are wise at an early age rarely live long. She is of course wrong, as this child will grow up to become the powerful King Edward III. In a perverse way, her remark is more appropriate to the foolish father than to the son. The threat of premature death hangs over numerous characters in this play, but not over Prince Edward. Isabella's remark could therefore be seen as another dramatic irony. Reactions to the news vary. Spencer objects to the ignoble means of the execution. Edward first thinks only of himself and weakly cannot decide how to react: 'O, shall I speak, or shall I sigh and die?' (line 122), a conventional-sounding line which could easily have come from a popular song of the time. Neither option seems particularly powerful, or practical. Spencer easily persuades Edward to act violently against the lords, and Edward picks up this suggestion in a bloodthirsty speech threatening **hyperbolic** levels of carnage.

If I be England's king, in lakes of gore
Your headless trunks, your bodies will I trail,
That you may drink your fill and quaff in blood,
And stain my royal standard with the same (lines 135–8).

Nevertheless, Edward's inherent weakness shows in his use of the conditional mood at the beginning of this speech: '*If* I be England's king' (line 135), a grammatical form which suggests doubt. Through this speech, Edward attempts to establish his story and that of Gaveston's death in an heroic and martial idiom, in turn inserted in an historical lineage. He inscribes himself in history. The dignified, formal tone is quite uncharacteristic of Edward, and shows not just how seriously he feels about this betrayal, but also his interpretation of it as an historically significant moment. In doing so, he forms a relationship between the personal (his own feelings) and the national (the projected suffering of the lords, enumerated in epic terms of manors and castles). Needless to say, Edward's fiction never becomes real. His words, though striking, are ineffectual (see also Textual Analysis, Text 2).

12 **Edward Longshanks** Edward I
13 **braves** challenges
14 **beard** accost
19 **counterbuffed of** dominated by
20 **preach on poles** if they were displayed on poles the severed heads of the nobles would carry a warning message to the people
27 **steel it on their crest** use steel (a sword) on their heads
28 **poll their tops** cut off their heads
haught high; noble
35 **of whence** from where
36-7 **bowmen and of pikes, / Brown bills and targeteers** various kinds of infantry
47 **Spencer** old Spencer, throughout this speech
57 **largess** gift of money
66 **Sib** shortened form of 'Isabella'
79 **towardness** early maturity
80 **marked** destined
127 **starting holes** dens
153 **iwis** I am sure

179 **Hie thee** hurry

181 **swell** develop an inflated opinion of themselves; also, collect more followers

183 **stoop** bow humbly

scene 12   **A battle takes place. Edward and the lords meet briefly and the battle continues**

Scene 12 begins with the battle promised at the close of Scene 11. Edward's side is retreating, but he wants them to attack. The older Spencer explains that both sides need some respite before fighting on. In the breathing space Edward and the Spencers encounter Mortimer, Lancaster, Warwick and Pembroke.

This scene begins with '*a great fight*' and the stage directions are clear that there must be a spectacular battle scene, with trumpets sounding ('*Alarums*') and charges ('*excursions*'). The damages envisaged in the previous scene are now enacted before our eyes. This kind of action scene was extremely popular with audiences and was often mentioned in the advertising for the printed editions of the play: it should take some minutes to perform, even though the instruction for it is easily missed by a reader. Within any protracted battle there are lulls and regroupings, such as Scene 12, and Marlowe uses that context to create a moment for personal confrontation. On a crowded stage the two parties exchange insults and threats, inflaming one another to fight on more fervently. Speech here carries on the action and contextualises it. Even after a long and exhausting fight, neither side will yield.

> Rather than thus be braved,
> Make England's civil towns huge heaps of stones
> And ploughs to go about our palace gates (lines 30–2).

Edward's frightening **rhetoric** suggests to Warwick that he has little awareness of his responsibilities to the country: 'A desperate and unnatural resolution' (line 33 – see Historical Background, on Nature/the Unnatural).

6 **either part** both sides

7 **breathe** rest

9 **retire** retreat

20 **Traitor on thy face** traitor yourself

SCENE 13   **Edward has won the battle and taken the rebels prisoner. Warwick and Lancaster are sent to execution and Mortimer to prison in the Tower**

Having triumphed in battle, Edward reiterates the reasons for his anger. Kent explains (yet again) that the purpose of Gaveston's death was to protect Edward and England. His argument is therefore that they are not traitors, even though they disobeyed the King's explicit command.

> KENT: Brother, in regard of thee and of thy land,
> Did they remove that flatterer from thy throne (lines 10–11).

All the lords view Edward as a tyrant who is damaging his country and needs to be stopped: Warwick calls him 'Tyrant' (line 21) and Mortimer calls him 'England's scourge' (line 38). Warwick and Lancaster, unrepentant, are taken away to execution. Kent is sent away and Mortimer is imprisoned in the Tower.

Edward departs, leaving Spencer and Levune. Spencer sends Levune to France to bribe the French nobility to remain neutral. He assumes that Isabella ('the subtle Queen' line 52) and the lords have plotted for a long time to join forces to control the King. Baldock objects, believing that the executions have already cancelled that plot. Levune, however, will persist in trying to bribe the King of France to ignore Isabella.

> This scene follows so smoothly from Scene 12 that in some editions it is treated as the same scene (in the Revels Plays edition they form Act III, Scene 2). Edward interprets his victory as demonstrating not that his side is stronger, but that they are in the right ('now not by chance of war / But justice of the quarrel and the cause' lines 1–2). He thus implicitly takes the medieval view of justice, that God assists the righteous to win.
>
> Edward's diction shows greater decision. 'Away!' (line 28) and 'Begone' (line 35) sound dominant, and his judgements on the noble prisoners are precisely differentiated according to the scale of each individual crime. For a moment the audience sees what Edward can be like when in power and undistracted by frivolities. When Mortimer's parting words call Edward 'England's scourge' (line 38), he implies that Edward is a tyrant who makes his people

suffer. His parting line claims that he has hope for a brighter future which is much greater than the bad luck he is currently experiencing: 'Mortimer's hope surmounts his fortune far' (line 39).

Advising Levune to bribe the French, Spencer inadvertently uses images of rape to describe Edward's career. Those who permit him to continue are like the guards who permitted Jove to rape Danaë (lines 46–8). This image together with the phrase 'showers of gold', based on **Ovid**, reminds us of the sensuous diction and the scholarly richness of reference used by Gaveston. It identifies Spencer as Gaveston's successor. How far we should see Spencer and Gaveston as images of an effete Renaissance learning, in opposition to the medieval machismo of the lords is a matter for debate.

This scene uses **alliteration** within lines, traditionally found in Old English and Middle English verse narrative. Examples are the reiterated 'p' in lines 17–18.

EDWARD: That thou, proud Warwick, watched the prisoner,
Poor Piers, and headed him against law of arms?

Line 31 alliterates on the consonant cluster 'gr' in 'Groan for this grief: behold how thou art maimed', and numerous other examples occur in the scene. One effect is to add to the sense that we are viewing a memorable, historic scene: the accusation of a tyrant by the people he is oppressing. A second effect is that this overtly poetic language draws attention to the status of the play as the self-conscious transmutation of Chronicle evidence into an art form.

3 **Vailed** bowed down

4 **we'll advance them** we will show off (your severed heads)

12 **avoid** leave

28 **vain** empty; worthless

38 **scourge** whip

48 **Danaë** in Greek mythology, she was a beautiful woman who was locked up by her father. The god Jove gained access to her by transforming himself into a shower of gold. The implication here is that the guards were bribed

51 **regiment** rule; control; discipline. This is **ambiguous**, as it may mean
that Prince Edward is to take over control of the realm from his father,
or (less likely) that the Prince will be returned to his father's control
53 **levelled at** aimed for
60 **amain** immediately

SCENE 14   **Kent helps Mortimer to escape from the Tower.**
            Together they leave for France

It is night. Kent, having been banished from court in the previous
scene, finds that the wind is set fair for France. He interprets this as a
sign that he should go there and help his country by joining Isabella ('the
wrongèd Queen' line 6). He sees the executions as 'unnatural' (line 8 – see
Historical Background, on Nature/the Unnatural). Kent has arranged to
meet Mortimer, who arrives having drugged his gaolers and escaped in
disguise. Kent has arranged their passage to France, and they leave
together.

We are not told where this scene is set, but it must be in London,
near the Tower and so also near the docks. Kent invokes Nature
as his support and as evidence that his departure for France
is a virtuous deed: the wind is 'fair' (line 1) which means both
'in the right direction' and 'beautiful', while 'gentle' (line 1) means
'noble' and 'honourable' (rather than the modern meaning of
'tender'). Edward, on the other hand, he represents as 'unnatural'
(line 8) in the sense of attacking one's own family or species (see
Historical Background, on Nature/the Unnatural). He also
encourages 'flatterers' (line 9) of such a radically different social
station that, in an important way, they do not count as belonging to
the same classification as Edward and the nobles. It is this
definition, of course, that Edward has resisted all along, believing
that he can ennoble his friends.

Far from feeling gratitude for being spared execution, Kent is angry
at being banished from the court. He sees his brother as 'proud'
(line 5) – one of the seven deadly sins. Much of the **diction**
surrounding Edward mimics the descriptions of tyrannical kings
from the Chronicles. To be proud, to surround oneself with

SCENE 14 continued

flatterers and to neglect one's country are all stereotypically tyrannical.

This scene shows the audience how Mortimer comes to be in France. Mortimer and Kent co-operate in their project, and the opponents of Edward gather strength. Dynamically, it matches the previous scene, in which the **theme** of evading gaolers has been mentioned by the opposition. It could therefore be taken to imply that the two sides use similar tactics.

SCENE 15 **Isabella and Prince Edward have difficulties in France and accept an offer of refuge in Hainault. Mortimer and Kent arrive and all depart for Hainault to gather forces for an attack on King Edward**

The forces of opposition to Edward begin to regroup abroad. When Isabella finds that there is no support for her position in France, her son suggests that they return to his father. She sees reconciliation as impossible. Fortunately, Sir John of Hainault offers friendship and they plan to stay in the Flemish county of Hainault. Kent and Mortimer arrive from England with ambitions to form an army. The Prince throughout is articulate, rational and honourable, distinguishing carefully between his father, whom he will not attack, and Spencer, whom he will. Mortimer and Kent believe that they could rally support within England (lines 54–6), with Mortimer the more warlike of the two. The scene closes with polite compliments to Sir John of Hainault.

The variety of different kinds of opposition to Edward is made clear in this scene. Prince Edward, appropriately, is the most reluctant to be involved in any attack on his father, but also feels strongly sympathetic towards his mother's problems. His first plan is to attempt yet another reconciliation between his parents, but Isabella is sadly aware that this is impossible. The dominant mood of the scene to begin with is one of sorrow and aimlessness. Sir John of Hainault seems involved on a personal level: he wishes to comfort the Queen in her distress. Hugely relieved to be offered a refuge, Isabella seems likely to live there until Prince Edward is older. When Mortimer and Kent arrive, the tone changes, and with it the pace of the action. Mortimer is all for planning an early invasion of

England. The Prince is doubtful. When it is suggested that it is his standard that Mortimer will advance, he objects that he will not lead an army against his father while the latter is alive 'How mean you, an the King my father lives?' (line 43). In other words, he does not consider himself to have any right to the crown until it comes to him in natural order of succession, on the death of his father (see Historical Background, on Nature/the Unnatural). The idea has now been planted in Isabella's mind, and with Mortimer's presence to give her courage, she seems to begin to see possibilities for an earlier return to England. Kent is passionately sorry for his country, which he sees as suffering under Edward's rule. He hopes that Edward will see reason, and reform himself. 'Would all were well and Edward well reclaimed, / For England's honour, peace, and quietness' (lines 57–8). Mortimer is convinced that only violent means will effect any changes. Thus, there is a clear gradation in the opinions of the members of the alliance against the King.

The sides are made clear within a **diction** which stresses friendship and support: Sir John asks Prince Edward 'How say you, my lord, will you go with your friends?' (line 19) and forms of the word 'friend' also occur at lines 1, 5, 35, 46, 47, 51, 54, 65, and 70. The executions are perceived as the loss of friends, while the King of France's friendship turns out to be worthless. Again, it is through networks of friends that information is passed: 'Monsieur le Grand, a noble friend of yours, / Told us at our arrival all the news' (lines 47–8). While others speak of friends and alliances, Mortimer refers consistently to the realities of doing battle: 'appointed for our foes' (line 56); 'by the sword' (line 59) and 'arms' (line 76).

1 **fail us** let us down

4 **a fig** a rude gesture

5 **my uncle** the King of France (Isabella's brother)

9 **be tuned together** be reconciled; musical **metaphors** such as 'harmony' or 'concord' for agreement between people are still used

10 **we jar** we are discordant; we argue

17 **Hainault** part of Flanders

30 **Tanaïs** 'the Latin name for the river Don, which the Elizabethans regarded as the boundary between Europe and Asia' (Wiggins & Lindsey)

SCENE 15 continued

32 **The Marquis** Sir John's brother William, who was Count of Hainault

40 **hap** luck

42 **t'advance your standard** to lead troops into battle on your behalf (under your flag)

52 **made away** killed

as such as

56 **appointed** armed and wearing armour, ready to do battle

57 **reclaimed** reformed (Wiggins & Lindsey give 'subdued', but Kent's wish that Edward might still be capable of good government makes more sense)

61 **ungentle** ignoble

66 **to bid the English King a base** to invite Edward to a trial of strength, as in a game

67 **match** contest, picking up the 'game' metaphor from the previous line

77 **anchor-hold** firm part of the sea-bed on which an anchor can grip; the 'anchor' is also an **emblem** of hope in conventional iconography

SCENE 16   **Edward celebrates his victory, but news arrives that Isabella, Mortimer, Kent and the young Prince Edward are collecting an army in Hainault. Edward leaves for Bristol to assemble his army**

Unaware of the plots brewing abroad, Edward and his court prepare to celebrate their victory and gloat over the list of people executed. He offers a reward for Mortimer's capture, confident that the latter is still in England. Letters arrive from Levune, reporting that Mortimer, Kent and the Queen are together. Edward curses them all and plans to meet them in battle. He spares a moment to regret that his young son has been swept into what he sees as wrongdoing.

In a scene echoing the previous one, we see the aftermath of the battle in England. Edward's court is a place of play-acting and of slippery instability. When line 2 asserts 'Triumpheth England's Edward with his friends', we recall that a triumph is a staged celebration, involving expense, costumes, often chariots and processions. Edward suggests misrule when he says that he will triumph 'with his friends uncontrolled' (line 3) and childishness in his rejection of authority as external. Edward's friends now have new titles: Spencer is addressed as 'My lord of Gloucester'. (Calling

Maltravers 'my lord of Arundel' may be another example of this, though editors differ. See Characterisation, on Maltravers.) This name change has a jarring effect of dislocation, as if these people are playing at being nobles and courtiers, changing names for fun as they would change their clothes. Identity under Edward is unstable, especially when at line 11 he slips back into calling Spencer by his original name. Edward has not really assimilated what a King is, namely a source of stability and control in his kingdom. Some of the sources on which stable authority is based appear in this scene in the form of documents: the list of the dead is based on a chronicle, the letter from Levune contributes information necessary to self-preservation. Edward, meanwhile, tends to destroy stability, and his reaction to threat is to rush off to Bristol.

The importance of Prince Edward continues to grow in a carefully controlled way. In the midst of Edward's anger and warlike preparations, Marlowe now has him spare a moment to think kindly of his son, whom he describes as a 'little boy' (line 49). In regretting that his son is misled (line 50), Edward unwittingly echoes his father's opinion of his own youthful relationship with Gaveston.

Finally in this highly balanced play, Edward's comment on the winds, associating them with both good and ill fortune, matches Mortimer's earlier remark (Scene 14, line 1). Living in a country that only three or four years before had seen the Armada dispersed by gales, Marlowe might well cause his characters to think of the winds as part of the arbitrary fortunes of war.

3 **triumph** a celebration of victory which became increasingly artistic and stylised over the years. It was based on the ancient Roman custom of parading prisoners through the streets
uncontrolled unhindered by authority

11 SPENCER [JUNIOR] *reads their names* clearly the list of names from **Holinshed** needs to be inserted at this point in performance. Wiggins & Lindsey print this list on p. 85; Forker locates it within the text and allocates line numbers accordingly

12 **'barked** embarked; set forth on a journey

SCENE 16 continued

18 **them can bring in Mortimer** those who can capture Mortimer

20 **A will be had ere long** he will be captured soon

41 **lead the round** lead the dance

43 **rout** unruly rabble

44 **Phoebus** the sun (a classical reference to the sun god whose chariot was said to pull the sun)

SCENE **17** **The army of Isabella, Mortimer and Prince Edward marches against Edward II**

The group of nobles has arrived back in England from Flanders (Hainault) with an army. In a pre-battle speech to inspire the army, Isabella regrets that the situation is necessary and begins to describe Edward's failings. Mortimer interrupts her with a brief clear statement. His plan is to restore the Queen to her position and banish the King's favourites.

The plot moves rapidly on, for within a very few minutes (in real time) since her despair in Scene 15, Isabella has arrived in strength in England. Many plays (notably Shakespeare's *Henry V*) contain speeches in which the leader of the army inspires the troops to fight. Isabella begins by punning on the idea of friends: 'kindest friends' (line 3) have been left in Belgium, while the 'friends at home' need to be 'coped with' i.e. confronted and defeated. She rehearses yet again the reasons why this military action is necessary, but Mortimer interrupts her with comic-**ironic** effect, for her speech is unnecessary both to the play and to the battle. It is gloomy and tedious, slowing matters down in both. Those who might want to stage this play for its laughs could find an opportunity here. Mortimer is much more politically pragmatic, using the Prince as an excuse to cover the treachery of their attack on the King.

Sir John jocularly purports to think that their war-trumpets will be mistaken for celebratory music. 'Edward will think we come to flatter him' (line 28). Kent answers, grounding the whimsy on a serious note, that he wishes this was the most flattery Edward had ever received.

SCENE 18   **Losing the war, the King is persuaded to flee to Ireland with Spencer and Baldock. Kent has second thoughts about betraying his brother the King. Spencer senior is captured and Mortimer arranges to have the King and his followers pursued**

In a scene near Bristol, the King's side is in panic. The stage direction, *'flying about the stage'*, brings the fear and urgency to a physical realisation. Against his sense of honour, Edward is persuaded by Spencer and Baldock to flee towards Ireland. Kent arrives on stage alone, leading the pursuit but well in advance of the other pursuers. His **soliloquy** reminds us that Edward is, after all, his brother. Kent has doubts about the legality of this attack on Edward, and sees himself as a traitor and 'unnatural' (line 18) because he has transgressed not just against the duty of subject to King, but of brother to brother (see Historical Background, on Nature/the Unnatural). He decides that he will conceal this opinion since Mortimer and Isabella have become involved in a love affair: 'Mortimer / And Isabel do kiss while they conspire' (lines 21–2). Though Isabella's concern for the King seems now to be completely spurious, it would also be possible to view her as fond of Edward at some contradictory level of consciousness.

Isabella, Mortimer, Prince Edward and Sir John of Hainault now enter. Isabella gives thanks to God for success in battle, and honours her son with the title 'Lord Warden' – suggesting that King Edward is incompetent to govern, and reversing the natural order whereby the father looks after the child. Kent is concerned to know what she plans to do with the King, calling him simply 'Edward' but Mortimer points out that it is a matter for Parliament to decide. Mortimer has noticed that Kent is softening towards Edward, and he and Isabella plot briefly in **asides**. They have already taken a merciless decision: all those caught fleeing the battlefield will be executed.

Kent's puzzling remark at line 54, 'This Edward is the ruin of the realm' has challenged scholars. It may be that Edward is speaking to himself, and mentally addressing his brother. 'This' therefore would refer to Baldock and the Spencers, who have just been mentioned. Alternatively, he may speak aloud, and simply be uttering the opinion that the others expect to hear, that Edward is the ruin of the realm.

Earlier scholars (such as Oxberry and Dyce) believed that Mortimer should speak the line.

Local people, including Rhys ap Howell and the Mayor of Bristol have taken Spencer senior prisoner and bring news that the King and his party have embarked for Ireland. Mortimer hopes for contrary winds to blow them back again. Kent is still genuinely regretful, while Isabella's self-justificatory sorrow seems hollow. Spencer senior is to be executed by decapitation since he is now a lord (lines 78–9). The scene closes with Mortimer giving instructions for the rebels to be pursued.

> For a brief space lasting nine lines only, we see the King and his party as they panic and flee. Edward is at first opposed to the dishonour of flight, claiming a sense of unified, permanent identity connected to his station in life: 'What, was I born to fly and run away?' (line 4 – see Themes, on Identity). Baldock's pragmatism ('this princely resolution / Fits not the time', lines 8–9) suggests that a person's behaviour is contingent on circumstances – slippery politics that Edward is rushed into accepting. By being so easily persuaded into flight, Edward is jumped into taking a decision which alienates him from his kingly self. Flight signifies changeability, which resembles insubstantial identity, and these manifest themselves as an inability to sustain himself as King. In this instant of decision, choosing lowly flight across the changeable sea instead of honourable death on horseback on the battlefield, Edward chooses without knowing it the ignominious course of events that will now follow. This sense of the absolute unretractability of some moments in one's life is part of what this play shows us and part of the point of its dominant mode of haste.

> The main focus in this scene, however, is on the King's brother, Kent, who now knows that he has taken a mistaken decision, and is keen to retract it.

> KENT: Edward, alas, my heart relents for thee.
> Proud traitor Mortimer, why dost thou chase
> Thy lawful King, thy sovereign, with thy sword?
> Vile wretch, and why hast thou of all unkind,
> Borne arms against thy brother and thy King? (lines 11–15).

Kent speaks in turn to Edward (line 11), to Mortimer (lines 12–13) and to himself. The **epithet** 'proud', typically applied to tyrants, is now used of Mortimer (also at line 27) and as Mortimer becomes more tyrannical, Kent sees his actions in a different light. He realises that Mortimer will not be satisfied until Edward is dead, and this is a step too far for Kent.

Isabella, victorious, is able to adopt the familiar view that success in battle is a sign of God's approval (lines 28–31). Naming her son Lord Warden of the kingdom gives him the custodial relationship with his people that his father so conspicuously neglects (see Historical Background, on Nature/the Unnatural).

Mortimer is clearly becoming more dominant. When Kent, the Prince and Isabella attempt to discuss the future, their conversation turns into a rather digressive meditation on what Edward is to be called. They perceive the significance of the confusion over his identity that lies at the heart of the play (see Themes, on Identity). Mortimer cuts the discussion short by denying that Isabella will have any say in the matter. It is he who takes decisions and gives instructions in this scene. He has the dominant function of uttering the closing words. The balance of power has shifted considerably since Mortimer was simply the rebel lord who was most sympathetic to Isabella.

_3_ **breathe** rest (from the battles)

_14_ **Vile wretch** Kent means himself

_25_ **Bristol** the Mayor of Bristol

Longshanks' blood the offspring of Edward I, i.e. King Edward II

_44_ **controlment** power

_60_ **Catiline of Rome** Roman politician c.108–62BC, renowned for his treachery to the state

_69_ **started** hunted out

_82_ **prates** talks nonsense

_85_ **runagates** renegades

SCENE 19   Still in England, Edward, Spencer and Baldock hide
with the Abbot and monks at the monastery at Neath.
The Mower has recognised them and they are arrested
by Rhys ap Howell and the Earl of Leicester

Having failed to reach Ireland, the King and his party are now in hiding
in Wales disguised as monks. The Abbot of Neath greets the royal
fugitives and assures them of his complete loyalty and secrecy. Edward
contemplates his fall from wealth and grandeur into his present
condition, and considers leading a life of learning and philosophy. These
would reconcile him to his fate. He fears that even the monks might
betray him for money. They reassure him, but Spencer feels that their
arrival was noticed by a labourer in the fields ('a gloomy fellow in a mead
below' – line 29). Baldock explains that bad weather prevented them from
reaching Ireland. Just as Edward, emotionally and physically exhausted,
entrusts himself to the Abbot, the Mower mentioned earlier enters with
Rhys ap Howell and the Earl of Leicester. They have an order for the
arrest of Spencer and Baldock. The King and his friends part in
passionate sorrow, Edward to captivity at Kenilworth Castle, the others
to execution. Edward leaves with Leicester. Spencer mourns the loss of
Edward while Baldock encourages him to think of heaven. The Mower
reminds ap Howell of his presence, apparently asking for the money he
has earned.

> This scene is remarkable for its complexity and compression. The
> information here is simple enough: Edward is captured and his
> friends are taken away to execution. More striking, however, is the
> poetic language in which these events and reactions to them are
> expressed. In an emotionally complex moment the fugitives are
> both panicky and also briefly at peace to contemplate their lives and
> try to make sense of what has happened.
>
> In a psychologically bizarre moment, Edward suggests that the
> Abbot imagine what it was like to be King, and from that to take
> pity on him.
>
> O hadst thou ever been a king, thy heart,
> Pierced deeply with sense of my distress,
> Could not but take compassion of my state (lines 9–11).

Projecting the concept of kingship on to others is so strange that we see how isolated it has made Edward. His own sense of self lacks boundaries. To Edward, it is the contrast between his previous glory and his present condition which is most poignant. Thus it is kingship itself which has made him so unhappy now.

Stately and proud, in riches and in train,
Whilom I was powerful and full of pomp;
But what is he, whom rule and empery
Have not in life or death made miserable? (lines 12–15).

Thus adopting a **topos** or **commonplace** from the theme of the fall of princes (see Literary Background, on The *de casibus* Tradition), Edward speaks as if he were already a *memento mori.*

Edward's next move is to resign himself to the present, and he plans to do this by studying ancient philosophers who taught how to live virtuously. In this dignified, reflective speech we see Edward for a while functioning as a true king. He has made space in which he can put his world into some kind of perspective. Even here, however, there is a dependence on others. In particular, the goodwill of the Abbot and monks is necessary to his survival. There are just too many observers in the world, and any one of them might give him away: Spencer has noticed someone looking at them suspiciously. Contemplation rapidly crumbles into jumbled anxieties when his fantasy world is broken into. This fragmentation of mood is imaged by the rapid to-and-fro of conversation between the monks, Spencer and Baldock, which jumps from one subject to another, until Edward longs for death. It is at that moment that death itself enters both **symbolically** and realistically. The anonymous Mower with a scythe-like 'Welsh hook' is a familiar image of death, while ap Howell and Leicester will take Edward to an imprisonment which will end in his death. The sight of Edward causes Leicester to pause and articulate the same topos that obsessed Edward earlier, namely the fall of princes from power (see Literary Background, on The *de casibus* Tradition). Unlike Gaveston, Spencer and Baldock are permitted to say their last farewells and resign themselves to death. Edward too sees nothing but death in his own future, though he still uses rather florid, literary language to describe it.

> Lay me in a hearse,
> And to the gates of hell convey me hence;
> Let Pluto's bells ring out my fatal knell,
> And hags howl for my death at Charon's shore,
> For friends hath Edward none but these, and these,
> And these must die under a tyrant's sword (lines 86–91).

Without his friends he sees himself as dead already. 'Life, farewell with my friends' (line 98). Such a comment suggests how necessary he found them to validate his own sense of self, or indeed of *being* at all.

Edward having departed with Leicester, Spencer is left to mourn his absence while Baldock, more practically, focuses on their own situation, advising prayer and cheerful thoughts of heaven. His generalisation, 'all live to die and rise to fall' (line 111) suggests that Edward's fall should be seen as exemplary of all human life and death. Such an interpretation is enhanced by the Mower's request to be remembered. Theatrically, he is already a *memento mori* and ap Howell's answer contains two meanings. He will remember the man's service by paying him his fee, and he will also, piously, remember that death is always present.

4 **fell** cruel, sudden

13 **Whilom** once; previously

16 **sit down by me** cf. Shakespeare's Richard II in similar circumstances 'for God's sake let us sit upon the ground, / And tell sad stories of the death of kings' (*Richard II*, III.2.151–2)

18 **nurseries of arts** institutions of learning

19 **Plato** ancient Greek philosopher whose teachings on ethical behaviour and on politics were highly thought of in the Middle Ages and Renaissance
Aristotle ancient Greek scientist and philosopher, author of the *Metaphysics*

27 **wot** know

29 **mead** meadow. The 'fellow' is there to mow the grass and make hay, suggesting that it is now summer

40 **mickle care** a great deal of worry

SCENE 19 continued

52 **reave** tear away

53–4 ***quem dies vidit veniens superbum, / Hunc dies vidit fugiens iacentum*** (Latin) 'He whom the dawning day saw in glory, the evening sees thrown down.' Leicester quotes the Roman tragedian Seneca

56 **by no other names** without using the titles given them by Edward

88 **Pluto's bells** a death knell that Edward imagines being rung by the ancient Greek god of the underworld

89 **Charon** in ancient Greek mythology, the ferryman who rowed dead souls across the river Styx in the underworld

112 **preachments** pious sentiments. Ap Howell chooses a term which sounds contemptuous

114 **wise work** ap Howell is being sarcastic. He means that their folly has wrecked the nation

SCENE 20   **Imprisoned at Kenilworth, Edward is asked to give up the crown to his son. He hesitates, but eventually gives way to the inevitable. He is moved from Kenilworth to Berkeley Castle**

The scene opens with the Earl of Leicester, the Bishop of Winchester, Trussel and King Edward all present. Leicester, officially Edward's gaoler and the lord of Kenilworth Castle, expresses a sympathetic attitude to Edward in his imprisonment. Edward is grateful but inconsolable and deeply angry with the adulterers Mortimer and Isabella. Powerless to achieve the revenge he imagines, he falls repeatedly into a rage: 'with the wings of rancorous disdain / Full often am I soaring up to heaven' (lines 20–1). This is followed by despair: 'sorrow at my elbow still attends / To company my heart with sad laments' (lines 33–4).

The Bishop of Winchester tries to persuade him to abdicate and pass the crown to his son, but Edward accurately sees this as a ruse by Mortimer to gain power. He is afraid that this would threaten his son: '[Prince Edward]'s a lamb encompassèd by wolves' (line 41). The more kindly disposed Leicester now puts pressure on Edward to come to a decision. Edward first accepts that he must hand over the crown, but delays through a last farewell, takes the crown off to look at it, puts it back on. Urged once again to decide, this time by Trussel, Edward becomes angry and insists that he will keep the crown as long as he lives.

The stage direction instructs '*The King rageth*' (line 85). Leicester utters the most persuasive idea of all:

> Call them again, my lord, and speak them fair,
> For if they go, the Prince shall lose his right (lines 91–2).

Only by abdicating can Edward ensure that his son will become king, rather than Mortimer. Edward, seeing the truth of this, relinquishes the crown, a gesture he sees as the annihilation of identity, or possibly even as death: 'Come death, and with thy fingers close my eyes, / Or if I live, let me forget myself' (lines 110–11). He sends a handkerchief wet with tears to the Queen, to **symbolise** his anguish. To his son he sends 'Commend me to my son and bid him rule / Better than I' (lines 121–2).

When Berkeley enters, Edward believes that this is his murderer: 'Come, Berkeley, come, / And tell thy message to my naked breast' (lines 129–30), but at this point Edward is to be moved to Berkeley Castle. In a parting gesture of friendship, Leicester is to travel with him for part of the journey.

As well as the more obvious external persuasion, Scene 20 involves a negotiation within Edward's own mind, as he gradually accepts that he must give up the crown. Leicester's sympathy enables Edward to explain his feelings in lengthy speeches. The protracted farewell to the crown echoes Edward's earlier farewells: the denied farewell to Gaveston, the achieved farewells to Spencer and Baldock. It is thus one in a sequence of three which may be viewed as stripping this man of everything he holds dear. Indeed, in losing these things Edward is stripped of identity, since he is constructed out of the trappings of self, and seems to have little or no secure internal identity. He describes kings without rule as 'perfect shadows in a sunshine day' (line 27) – a shadow is entirely dependent on the external agency of the sun for its very existence, something that vanishes when the weather clouds over. The 'sun' can be read as a **metaphor** for popular approval. There is, I will argue later, a final deprivation still to come for Edward (see Themes, on Loss).

Delay with a clearly fixed term ('But stay awhile; let me be King till night' line 59) is also strongly reminiscent of Faustus's last hours on earth before descending into Hell, at the end of Marlowe's most famous play, *Dr Faustus*. Like Faustus, Edward commands time to stop.

Stand still, you watches of the element;
All times and seasons rest you at a stay,
That Edward may be still fair England's King (lines 66–68).

In the first portion of the scene Edward repeatedly invokes animal **imagery** to interpret his situation. At lines 9–12 he images himself as a wounded lion, reacting with rage and dignity in contrast to ordinary people, imaged as deer whose wounds are easily healed. Next he pictures himself with wings which enable him to fly up to heaven to obtain justice. His son too he sees in victimised terms as a lamb amongst predatory wolves, by whom he means Mortimer. Later he sees Mortimer and Isabella as 'inhuman creatures' (line 71) who have been raised by tigers and so have become 'monsters' (line 74). The metamorphoses he envisages derive from **Ovidian** violence: not only are people monsters, but Isabel's eyes are 'turned to steel' (line 104) and 'sparkle fire' (line 105). Edward, meta-morphosing from a king to something he cannot imagine except as death, now sees much of the rest of the world in metamorphic terms.

The use of three advisers to persuade Edward is dramatically effective, suggesting as it does a crowd of people all trying to make Edward do something he wants to avoid. As representatives of the nobility (Leicester), the Church (Bishop of Winchester) and the ordinary people (Trussel), they function **emblematically** of the nation as a whole. On stage, Edward's isolation becomes obvious, and in spite of his lengthy speeches, clearly he cannot long avoid giving up the crown.

One effect of Edward's many reversals of opinion in this scene is that we in the audience cease to believe that he means what he says. We no longer know where the truth lies, and so to some extent share Edward's own instabilities. When Berkeley explains that he is loyal to the King and will not kill him, we cannot be sure whether

Scene 20 continued

to trust him or not. Edward of course has no choice, and now comforts himself with the thought of death.

Throughout the scene the word 'must' recurs with increasing force and poignancy, as Edward uses it to show how unaccustomed he is to taking orders. Petty though this may seem, it is fundamental to his concept of himself as a king. Some degree of autonomy is also fundamental to a human being's sense of identity, and the reiterated imperatives can therefore be felt as intrusive, even outrageous, by any one of us. As Edward loses his identity, in his own mind it becomes something that he can pass on to his son, who inherits both his name and the kingship. When Edward is anxious that his son will survive to be king, he protects a little of himself.

5 **gentle** noble; courteous

26 **regiment** rule

33 **sorrow at my elbow still attends** sorrow is **personified** as a servant who is always present, singing to him

45 **Tisiphon** in ancient Greek mythology, Tisiphone was one of the Furies: fiendish women whose task was to be revenged on the guilty by pursuing them endlessly. Their terrifying appearance included snakes for hair

51 **weigh how hardly I can brook** consider with what difficulty I can bear

66 **watches of the element** sections of the night; the stars appear to move as time passes

77 **They pass not** they do not care

84 **present** immediate

109 **for aye** for ever

133 **devoir** (French) duty

SCENE 21   **Mortimer and Queen Isabella receive the crown. Mortimer arranges for Edward to be more cruelly and secretly imprisoned by Gourney and Maltravers. Kent now supports the King and suspects Mortimer and Isabella of foul play. His attempts to protect Prince Edward from them fail and he plans to free the King**

Mortimer expounds his plans to Isabella. Having executed the King's followers, he now wants to take firmer control by having Prince Edward made King and himself Protector. Isabella gives Mortimer permission to do what he thinks best with the King. At this point, the crown is brought from Kenilworth. Mortimer feels threatened that Edward still has many friends, including Leicester and Kent. He fears that an escape would cause more warfare.

Two bully-boys, Gourney and Maltravers, are appointed as Edward's gaolers and given explicit instructions to move him from one place to another in as uncomfortable a manner as possible. Mortimer has thus licensed a kind of torture, and clearly hopes that Edward will die of maltreatment. Mortimer envisages psychological as well as physical torment, insisting that Edward should never be spoken to in a friendly or comforting manner. Isabella deceitfully sends a sympathetic message and a gift, perhaps to conceal her involvement in the plot.

As Gourney and Maltravers leave, Prince Edward enters with Kent. Kent quickly sees through Isabella and Mortimer's charade of sympathy towards Edward. Mortimer suggests that Kent should be Protector, Kent suggests Isabella, and Prince Edward would prefer his father to remain king until he himself is old enough to reign. The discussion quickly descends into a violent argument, concluded when Mortimer seizes the protesting prince and rushes off with him, followed by Isabella. This leaves Kent alone to close the scene with his plans to rescue Edward from Kenilworth Castle and to be revenged on Mortimer and Isabella.

In a revelational scene that moves the plot swiftly onwards, we are shown Mortimer and Isabella in their true colours. They are indeed the cruel villains that Edward perceives them to be. Where the previous scene contained lengthy monologues of poetic and passionate intensity, this scene offers a complete contrast. Once Mortimer's opening speech is over, the scene consists largely of brief, pointed conversations in which key information is presented and the speakers reason with one another. Isabella's hypocrisy is made clear, while Mortimer, once in possession of the crown and of Isabella's acquiescence now feels safe to maltreat Edward and hasten his death, with Gourney and Maltravers as his thuggish accomplices. Mortimer uses the traditional image of Fortune's wheel to describe his rapidly increasing power (see Literary Background, on The *de casibus* Tradition). This image of a huge

Scene 21 continued

turning wheel to which everyone is tied signified that one's luck could always change. Mortimer arrogantly sees himself in control of the wheel, a level of **hubris** which signals disaster: 'Mortimer, / Who now makes Fortune's wheel turn as he please' (lines 51–2). Rumours that Edward still has supporters and that Kent is plotting to free him seem to justify Mortimer in inflicting further disorientation on the King. In England, where locations have been precisely specified, Edward no longer even knows *where* he is. Like other tyrants, Mortimer increasingly surrounds himself with people of low social position and low morals, such as Gourney and Maltravers. His own villainy shows more clearly as, according to popular wisdom, like consorts with like. Edward, on the other hand, now attracts the friendship of peers who once fought against him, including his brother Kent.

13 **behoof** orders

14 **underwrit** written underneath (signed)

17 **so** as long as

37 **privy seal** a royal seal attached to certain documents as proof that they are issued by royal authority

39 **drift** plot

57 **casts** plans

73 **dissembled** lied

81 **enlarged** set free

103 **not meet** not fitting; inappropriate

110 **'sdain'st** disdainest

SCENE 22 **Maltravers and Gourney transport King Edward from one filthy dungeon to the next. On the way they shave him in a puddle before arriving at Kenilworth Castle. Kent attempts to contact the King, but is captured and taken to Mortimer's court**

Set at night, Scene 22 acts out the results of the instructions Mortimer gave in the previous scene, with Maltravers and Gourney pretending to be Edward's friends while forcing him to travel from one prison to the next. Edward, in his spiritual and physical misery, recognises that Mortimer and Isabella want him dead and now considers that death would be a welcome release. He asks for clean water, but is given water from a ditch. Gourney and Maltravers proceed to wash and shave him in this stagnant water – an action both humiliating and painful. As they approach Kenilworth castle, Kent attempts to speak to Edward and possibly even to save him. Instead Kent is speedily captured. He laments the topsy-turvy nature of a world where a mere noble like Mortimer can be referred to as having a 'court', while the King is imprisoned. Kent resigns himself to despair and death.

> Dramatic tension is sustained as Mortimer's plan in Scene 21 carries directly on to its realisation in Scene 22. Edward's misery is made clear, and the animal he feels most affinity with now is the owl: 'the nightly bird / Whose sight is loathsome to all wingèd fowls' (lines 6–7). At line 34 he identifies with the wren, as an image of weakness.
>
> Edward begs for death only to be offered lies: a further refinement of mental torment, since the dissonance between experienced reality and the words he is offered is both insulting and confusing. In a recurrence of the **theme** of 'foul water', Edward's shaving in a ditch recalls both Gaveston's unceremonious beheading in a ditch (between Scenes 10 and 11), and his own rude treatment of the Bishop of Coventry in Scene 1 (see Narrative Technique). Edward here sees his shaving as part of a reparation for the death he brought on Gaveston: 'For me, both thou and both the Spencers died, / And for your sakes a thousand wrongs I'll take' (lines 42–3).
>
> If anything, however, these painful events seem to make Edward stronger. He has survived hunger, imprisonment, neglect and poisonous physical conditions in remarkably good health. He has a clearer view than ever before of where truth lies, shown by his capacity to contradict Gourney's lie in line 15 with the truth in line 16.
>
> GOURNEY: Your passions make your dolours to increase
> EDWARD: This usage makes my misery increase (lines 15–16)
>
> He also understands how his behaviour has led to the deaths of his friends and the nature of the moral imperatives that sheer *being* has

placed on him. He explains clearly why he must struggle, even though it is pointless to do so.

MALTRAVERS: Why strive you thus? Your labour is in vain.

EDWARD: The wren may strive against the lion's strength,

But all in vain; so vainly do I strive

To seek for mercy at a tyrant's hand (lines 33–36).

The concept that one must plead even when it is doomed to failure seems to have been well known in the early 1590s. It reappears in Shakespeare's *Titus Andronicus* (III.1.34–6, in *The Oxford Shakespeare: The Complete Works* ed. Wells & Taylor, 1986).

Edward has found a common human experience through his suffering.

6 **the nightly bird** the owl

10 **unbowel** disembowel; remove the vital organs

12 **the chiefest mark** the main target

52 **thrust in the King** push the King into (the dungeon)

63 **commonweal** country; way of running the state

SCENE 23   Still determined that Edward's death is necessary to preserve his own position, Mortimer employs a hireling, Lightborne, to commit the murder. An experienced murderer, Lightborne carries an ambiguously punctuated letter to Maltravers which could be read as permitting him to kill the King, or forbidding it. Mortimer gloats over his position as Protector. The coronation of Prince Edward as King Edward III takes place with due ceremony. The captive Kent is brought in, and Mortimer and Edward III clash over his fate. Mortimer succeeds in having Kent taken away to execution. Edward III reflects on his own position

This scene begins with Mortimer alone, revealing through **soliloquy** his plans for Edward's immediate death. Behaving increasingly like a **Morality Play Vice**, Mortimer uses the **ambiguities** inherent in Latin **syntax** to conceal his role in the murder of Edward. Mysteriously the letter is 'written by a friend of ours' (line 6) – a reference which is never explained. Mortimer must, of course, appear to be innocent of any crime if he is to retain power in the kingdom. He has ensured that Lightborne will in turn be murdered to preserve the secrecy of his hand in the plot.

Lightborne, whose name is a broad English translation of Lucifer, is an appropriately devilish agent for Mortimer to use. He boasts of his skill in secret killing but refuses to divulge how he plans to kill Edward. Lightborne departed, Mortimer's soliloquy shows his love of power and of the violence which the possession of power encourages in his imagination. He richly enjoys the deception with which he has pretended to be inadequate to the role of Protector but then succumbed to persuasion. The point for him is one of control: that no-one should control him, while he has absolute control over others. With consummate dramatic economy, Mortimer's closing remark that today is the coronation day merges into a fanfare of trumpets and the coronation procession.

The newly crowned Edward III, with the Bishop of Coventry, the nobles, Queen Isabella and Mortimer form an impressive procession. In a ceremony of great antiquity the Bishop announces the coronation, and the King's Champion then offers to do battle against anyone who does not accept Edward III's coronation. Like other ceremonial challenges, this goes unanswered, the trumpets sound again, and the King drinks a toast to the Champion.

Kent is now brought in and arraigned as a traitor for having attempted to release his brother Edward II. Against Edward III's objections and pleas, Mortimer is adamant, and Kent, protesting, is dragged off to be executed.

Alone with his mother, the young King Edward is quick to perceive that Mortimer could be a threat to his own life.

A varied scene, involving dark plots, glorious ceremony and a clash of wills makes Mortimer's tyranny public not just to the audience, but also to the new King, Edward III. Mortimer does not want power in order to put forward any particular programme since his earlier aim to curb Edward's expenditure has presumably now been amply achieved. Mortimer's mad craving for autonomy is in some ways a mirror image of Edward's own perception of the personal consequences of kingship: to be able to control, while avoiding being controlled.

Now all is sure: the Queen and Mortimer
Shall rule the realm, the King, and none rule us.
Mine enemies will I plague, my friends advance,
And what I list command, who dare control? (lines 63–6).

This attitude might well be compared with Edward's earlier line, 'And triumph Edward with his friends uncontrolled' (Scene 16, line 3). Mortimer has come to enjoy the effects of exercising power (lines 46–55), while maintaining the appearance of reluctance to govern, and relishing the skill with which he maintains the deceit (lines 56–61). The terms he uses, including the repeated use of 'I' (lines 46–51) smack of **hubris** and anticipate his imminent fall. Mortimer uses Latin phrases to describe his deceptions, an effect which evokes suspicion of the scholarly and a fear of the deceits that clever individuals might devise. Yet it is also an effect which rebounds against him, since he seems to have learned nothing morally worthwhile for all his education.

The coronation that follows shows Mortimer's appropriation of the pomp and ceremony of the court, and his stage-management of the young King. (Edward III was in fact fifteen when he succeeded his father in 1327.) It is Mortimer who instructs the trumpeters, and Mortimer to whom Isabella formally hands over responsibility for her son. The complex plot is held tightly together by the arrival of Kent under guard, having been taken prisoner in Scene 22 at Kenilworth. At this point there is a clear sense that Mortimer and Edward III are jockeying for position in the conversation. The **stichomythia** of their exchange (lines 84–9) dramatises the intensity of the confrontation. Edward III, now anything but passive, clearly wishes to be involved in decision-making, but Kent's fate is taken out of his hands. Taking in this object lesson in power, the boy King perceptively realises how dangerous Mortimer might become. When Edward III forms an independent judgement of events by defining Kent's fate as 'murder' (line 107), this contrasts with Isabella, who echoes Mortimer's decision that Kent is 'a

traitor' (line 112). Edward III achieves a level of mature moral
autonomy suggestive of his future power. He refuses to forget Kent:
'And shall my uncle Edmund ride with us?' (line 111). Isabella's
reassurances and offers of childish distractions are neither credible
nor appropriate.

8 ***Edwardum occidere nolite timere, bonum est*** (Latin) Do not be afraid to kill
Edward, it is good (*comma inserted*)

11 ***Edwardum occidere nolite, timere bonum est*** (Latin) Do not kill Edward, it is
good to be afraid (*comma inserted*)

13 **Unpointed** unpunctuated (notice the positions of the comma)

18 **perform the rest** do the murder

21 **Lightborne** a rough translation of 'Lucifer', which is the name of the Devil in
Christian mythology

23 **cast** planned

26 **I use much to relent** (sarcastic) I'm used to relenting

27 **bravely** cleverly; boldly

31 **lawn** fine cotton or linen. Explaining this method has challenged editors.
Most believe it to refer to a method of choking the victim silently

35 **quicksilver** mercury

42 **never see me more** Mortimer accidentally speaks the truth: Lightborne *will*
never see him because Lightborne will be dead. He picks up on this in the
next line, and Mortimer covers with a lie at line 44

47 **congé** (French) bow; in modern French a *congé* is a holiday

52 **Aristarchus** a schoolmaster in ancient Alexandria, famous for his brutal
methods of discipline

53 **breeching** beating

57 **Puritan** a member of a Protestant religious group in the sixteenth century

59 ***onus quam gravissimum*** (Latin) a burden which is too heavy

61 ***Suscepi*** that ***provinciam*** (Latin and English mixed) a **macaronic** phrase
meaning I have taken on that area of duty

67 ***Maior sum quam cui possit fortuna nocere*** (Latin) I am so great that Fortune
is not able to harm me

79 **blades and bills** swords and halberds (**metonymic**)

94 **methinks** I imagine; I dream

SCENE 24   **The gaolers Gourney and Maltravers find that they cannot force Edward's death by neglect and natural causes. Lightborne arrives and they provide him with the instruments of torture he requests. In the dungeon itself he first comforts Edward with conversation, then murders him. Gourney murders Lightborne, and he and Maltravers take the body of Edward to Mortimer**

At Berkeley Castle, Maltravers and Gourney discuss Edward's condition. Although imprisoned in a dungeon containing the castle's effluent run-off, he remains physically healthy. Clearly they had hoped to avoid any blame for murdering him by ensuring that he would fall ill and die in the bad conditions. Just as they decide to embark on further mental torture, Lightborne arrives with the coded messages. The Latin phrase baffles Gourney, but the better-educated Maltravers interprets both it and the additional 'token' (line 19) which tells them to murder Lightborne afterwards. The atmosphere darkens further when we hear what Lightborne requires: a red-hot spit (or poker), a table and a feather mattress. Gourney, again the slower-witted of the two, cannot understand the method of killing, and asks 'That's all?' (line 34).

Lightborne converses with Edward, lying to him about his reason for being there and claiming that he has come to bring comfort. Edward details his pathetic circumstances and Lightborne cunningly persuades him to lie down and sleep on the palliasse he has brought. In reality he wants to get Edward into a reclining position where he can be crushed with the table and spitted with the red-hot poker. In this way, Lightborne will have shed no blood, and no evidence of the murder will be observable on the body. Edward, however, imagines death as quick, a 'stroke' (line 75), presumably of a knife or a sword. He wishes to see it coming and to focus on God: neither of these things will happen. Lightborne persuades him that it is safe to fall asleep.

Now begins the most extraordinary and shocking part of this (or any) play, when Lightborne, Gourney and Maltravers press Edward under the table, and use the hot spit to perform a hellish sodomy that eventually kills him. Maltravers's line 'I fear me that this cry will wake the town' (line 113) indicates that Edward's screams are extremely loud and prolonged. Once Edward is dead, Lightborne is quickly murdered and his body unceremoniously thrown into the castle moat.

Edward's body is taken to Mortimer. Because he has died of internal injuries there will be no evidence of murder on the body.

> LIGHTBORNE: So, lay the table down and stamp on it;
> But not too hard, lest that you bruise his body (lines 111–12).

Confined in the horrors of the dungeon, Edward is at his most pitiable. The dungeon is an image of hell: **symbolically** through its position low down in the castle, and also because it is stinking, dark, noisy and confused. Edward himself fears that he may be losing his mind.

Lightborne's comforting words are clearly lies, and confuse Edward further. It is not just Latin that is to be mistrusted, but any language that is offered to Edward. Nevertheless, Edward's own speech is clear, detailed and deeply poignant. He has lost everything: friends, status, kingship and any normal human sustenance or surroundings. Very briefly he recalls happier days when he courted Isabella, but seems incapable of understanding how his own behaviour has made her into an enemy. All he has left is the knowledge of death and faith in God. He has several times already mentioned these as the final comfort (Scene 19, lines 41–3; Scene 20, lines 110–11), and now does so again.

> And let me see the stroke before it comes,
> That even then when I shall lose my life,
> My mind may be more steadfast on my God (lines 75–6).

Edward is still imagining that the end to his life can be controlled and rational (see Themes, on Loss). Lightborne takes even this from him: compressed under a table he cannot 'see the stroke', nor will it be a single clean blow with a knife or sword. Finally, his dying screams suggest he could not think of God while he died in agony. Edward thus has fallen below any standard of deprivation envisaged by the *de casibus* tradition (see Literary Background, on The *de casibus* Tradition). In the Synopsis I referred to this play as involving a series of losses. Now Edward has lost what none of his followers lost: the chance to prepare himself to die. The *memento mori* of the Mower who appeared to Spencer is relatively gentle in comparison to the lying fiend Lightborne.

This scene is one of reversals and contradictions, where not only is language perverted (in the death-message) and religion mocked (in Lightborne's diabolical reversal of the priestly role, offering lies as comfort), but the kind of death a King might expect is made grotesque and tortured. Instead of beheading or a sword-blow in battle, Edward's body is outraged by the torment of having his bowels burnt away via the anus. Notoriously, according to Holinshed, his screams could be heard for miles.

The water **theme** now reappears (see Narrative Technique). Where Gaveston's death in a ditch (reported in Scene 11, lines 119–20) was echoed by Edward's shaving (Scene 22) and his incarceration in sewage, Lightborne's body is also dumped in the filthy anonymity of the castle moat (Scene 24). This should not be seen as a recompense for Edward's death, so much as a repetition in a different key of the 'pride before a fall' theme.

8 **meat** food

9 **savour** stink

16 **unpointed** unpunctuated

for the nonce for now

17 ***Edwardum occidere nolite timere*** (Latin) Do not be afraid to kill Edward (see note, Scene 23)

24 ***Pereat iste!*** (Latin) Let him die!

25 **lake** dungeon

38 **this gear** this plan (a typical **Vice** phrase)

51 **List** listen

53 **Caucasus** a mountain range made of solid rock

55 **sink** sewer; cess-pit

68 **ran at tilt** jousted

73 **tragedy** the conclusion of the story: death

91 **overwatched** overtired from lack of sleep

113 **raise** wake; rouse

SCENE 25   **Maltravers reports to Mortimer and flees. Edward III has discovered what has happened and condemns Mortimer to death by hanging. He has Isabella imprisoned in the Tower, and arranges his father's funeral. Edward III is now in complete control**

Again, time is elided, and we immediately see Maltravers reporting to Mortimer and expressing his regret at the deed. Gourney has fled and Maltravers follows him. Mortimer sees himself as invincible and the murder as secret, but Isabella enters, having already heard a rumour of the murder from another source. King Edward III, supported by the remaining lords, now condemns Mortimer to death. As evidence he has the **ambiguous** Latin letter, which he has no difficulty in understanding. Mortimer believes he cannot be condemned without the evidence of Lightborne, but Edward III cuts through this with a command that his own knowledge is sufficient. Mortimer is to be hanged and quartered, and he resigns himself to this. His parting speech contains an explicit statement that he has risen on the wheel of Fortune to the peak, and now must continue the journey downwards. His courageous last words suggest an adventurous, even atheistic, spirit in which he sees himself as 'a traveller' who 'goes to discover countries yet unknown' (lines 65–6).

Edward III deals abruptly with his mother, refusing to listen to her pleas for Mortimer, but showing filial loyalty by sending her to imprisonment in the Tower rather than executing her as well. He refuses to let her participate in his father's funeral. The play closes with the solemn pageantry of the funeral procession, adorned with Mortimer's head, and Edward III speaks in a dominant if sorrowful mode of his own grief and regret.

> Like all tyrants, Mortimer finds that even his henchmen cannot tolerate his extremes and are deserting him. He becomes increasingly boastful and overconfident, in contrast to the statesmanlike Edward III. The latter demonstrates his kingly qualities by his strong sense of justice, his ability to rally support and his capacity to see through the deceits of the Latin death-letter.

> Mortimer's closing lines are duly impressive for such a major villain and inheritor of the stage tradition of the **Vice**. He sees himself as

a victim of the inevitability of chance – that one's Fortune may rise but it must also fall. He curses Fortune as 'base', presumably for betraying him.

> Base Fortune, now I see that in thy wheel
> There is a point to which, when men aspire,
> They tumble headlong down; that point I touched,
> And seeing there was no place to mount up higher,
> Why should I grieve at my declining fall?
> Farewell, fair Queen. Weep not for Mortimer,
> That scorns the world, and as a traveller
> Goes to discover countries yet unknown (lines 59–66).

Mortimer's pride is never humbled, nor does he ever express repentance. He goes to his death with scorn for the world.

Edward III has no hesitation in imposing summary justice of an effective and highly **symbolic** nature. Furthermore, he is instantly obeyed. Placing Mortimer's severed head on Edward II's hearse will speak unequivocally to all who see it, while the quartered body, displayed at key parts of the kingdom, will transmit the message even more broadly. That message conveys not just Mortimer's guilt, but also Edward III's capacity to deal with the threat of misrule. Edward III has taken on his father's role and his father's cause ('in me my loving father speaks' line 41) but not his father's follies.

The play ends, then, with the realm cleansed both of Edward II's profligacy and of Mortimer's plots, and with a potentially admirable and competent king on the throne.

11 **Jove's huge tree** the oak
52 **hurdle** sledge or frame
90 **boots** matters

PART THREE

CRITICAL APPROACHES

THEMES

ENGLAND

Even more than many other **history plays**, *Edward II* ranges over the length and breadth of England and displays a wide range of social classes (see Characterisation). The late sixteenth century was a time when 'the matter of Britain' was of particular interest: a period when Englishness and national pride were being defined. Marlowe's play participates actively in this process. The scene moves from London to Tynemouth in the North, to Cobham in Kent (where Gaveston is murdered), to Neath in Wales and to Kenilworth in the Midlands, and finally to Berkeley Castle. The barons are strongly identified with the counties or cities from which they come – Warwick, Lancaster, Leicester, and so on. When they mock Gaveston's new titles (Scene 6), part of their outrage seems to stem from this Frenchman's acquisition of England in segments: Earl of Cornwall, Lord of Man (the Isle of Man) and Bishop of Coventry. Edward has apparently given him portions of the realm as love tokens.

Edward's personal story is entirely contained within England: he seems to be powerless to leave. We hear that his campaign against the Scots is humiliatingly turned back, while the flight to Ireland is prevented by fatefully bad weather. Traversing the length and breadth of England, Edward in his **tragedy** treads the bounds of his kingdom. The treacherous enemies of Edward (and arguably of Englishness) are in many cases characterised as foreign. Isabella, for example, is French, while Mortimer identifies his background as French, or Francophone (Mortimer, or *mort de mer*, means the Dead Sea: Scene 7, lines 21–3). Mortimer's foreignness is characterised as political astuteness, dedicated anger and intelligent ambition. He is also viciously resentful. The alliance against Edward is forged in exile, and facilitated by the supportive Sir John of Hainault.

The geographical space is populated by a particularly large range of minor characters, part of whose dramatic function is to display the rich variety of social classes whose lives are affected by Edward's behaviour and bad government. The angry barons are served by numerous gentlemen, horse-boys and soldiers, not to mention gaolers and even the hired murderer, Lightborne. The middle classes appear in the persons of the Mayor of Bristol and Trussel, while the presence of Rhys ap Howell displays Wales as part of the realm. All levels of priests make an appearance, from the Bishop of Canterbury down to simple monks. Meanwhile, Edward's court contains gentlemen, both upper (the Spencers) and lower (Baldock), civil officials (the Clerk of the Crown) and servants (the 'Post'). Anonymous ordinary people have significant roles: the Three Poor Men and the Mower. Numerous other unnamed figures such as guards and soldiers keep the structures of the world running, and we sense that we are seeing as complete a picture of society as possible (but see Critical History, on Feminism).

One could argue that Edward falls because he fails to care for England and its people, but encourages a kind of foreignness inside himself. It is yet another foreigner – Gaveston – who sets him on this track, through his exotic shows and pretences. The conclusion of this trajectory of the play is to leave us with a fortress England, purged of foreign influence by the deaths of Mortimer and Gaveston, and incarceration of Isabella. Power is held by an unequivocally English king, Edward III, who identifies himself with his father: 'Traitor, in me my loving father speaks / And plainly saith, 'twas thou that murd'redst him' (Scene 25, lines 41–2). The young King **symbolically** cuts away his French heritage when he imprisons his mother in the Tower. England in this play, then, is defined emotionally and morally in opposition to the foreign; geographically as an amalgam of regions, and in human terms, as a comprehensive variety of social classes.

IDENTITY

At the heart of the play is Edward's troubled identity: as a man, as a king and as a father. He is so easily swayed by his favourites (who automatically become his advisers) that he appears to have little will of his own. Indeed, he has little sense of any boundaries to identity, seeing himself as somehow the same person as Gaveston ('Thy friend, thy self, another Gaveston!' – Scene 1, line 142). He only feels real when

Gaveston is with him, and mourns passionately when Gaveston is absent. Insecurity of identity is imaged by his taste for shows and play-acting, all of which offer a fictitiously delightful world where a person can adopt any identity he likes. It is significant of his confusion between appearance and reality that the public attempt to enforce his will by fighting the Scots is conducted with Edward almost in disguise, and his troops dressed like actors. 'Thy soldiers marched like players' (Scene 6, line 180). Edward dresses up as the heterosexual king that he is not, and is met by reality when he is ingloriously defeated in battle (Scene 6, lines 185–6).

Edward understands that his status as a king confers privileges, and that it has the potential to structure a kind of identity. In general though, his attempts at dominance fail: he utters blustering orders and threats that are disobeyed. His one attempt at kingly courage on a battlefield is thwarted by bad advice to flee (Scene 18, lines 1–9). Recognising his inadequacy as a king, the motif of wanting to separate himself from the normal world reappears on several occasions. In Tynemouth, for example, Edward plays with the idea of living in quiet seclusion, and forlornly returns to this theme at the Abbey of Neath. When he finally faces death, he is left with very little, and has no inner resources on which to call. He depends upon 'the kindness of strangers' (to quote Tennessee Williams, *A Streetcar Named Desire*) but in his case that reliance is hollow.

Loss

(See also Narrative Structures.) Edward's fall involves his attempts to shore up his identity by surrounding himself with favourites, each of whom he loses, at first temporarily and then finally. Yet when his friends Gaveston and Spencer are dead and his royal powers have all been stripped away, we find that Edward still retains some sense of self. In Scene 24 he realises that the name of king as symbolised by the crown still means a great deal. He cannot imagine life without it, which suggests that his identity is profoundly invested in his kingship. Where previously he has referred to classical myths, and to classical ideas of hell as an underworld, when he gives up the crown he turns to a Christian God and to traditional concepts of the worthlessness of worldly things.

> Now, sweet God of heaven,
> Make me despise this transitory pomp,
> And sit for aye enthronizèd in heaven,
> Come death, and with thy fingers close my eyes,
> Or if I live, let me forget myself (Scene 20, lines 107–11).

At this point he seems to see death as merciful, and comforts himself with the thought of it. He expresses several beliefs about death. Even this last concept will soon be taken from him, in a scene of ultimate loss – not simply of his life, but of his faith in the nature of death. This becomes obvious when one compares Edward's expectations with the events that unfold. He speaks almost lightly of death in Scene 22, at lines 24, 44–5 and 66. In Scene 24, speaking to Lightborne, he anticipates a quick end:

> And let me see the stroke before it comes,
> That even then when I shall lose my life
> My mind may be more steadfast on my God (lines 75–7).

Contrary to his vision, there will be far more than a single 'stroke', he will not be able to see it, and he will not be able to fix his mind upon God. The infamous nature of Edward's tortured, screaming, protracted death was so well known that his words about death already ring hollow to anyone who hears or reads them. Contemporary audiences of Marlowe's play were well aware of the circumstances, even though Edward's death had taken place over 250 years earlier. In this way, I argue that Edward suffers his final and most profound loss: a loss of his faith in the comfort of death.

CHARACTERISATION

This section contains a brief discussion of characterisation in general, then of each of the characters in the play, with additional observations about the possibilities for alternative interpretations in performance. Beside each character there is a note of the scenes where that character appears. A list like this helps to show which characters are never on stage at the same time as one another and so can be **doubled** in performance.

A play is designed to be performed and so completing the form of each of the characters requires a real person to act the part, bringing to it all the quirks of personal appearance, mannerisms and tones of voice that the actor already possesses. These must be coherent with the part as written, but they also (literally) flesh it out. In this way, the genre of the play text needs to be read with the added consciousness of the possibilities it provides for performance. Considering each character separately allows us to ask ourselves what can be made of each word, and what it might imply about the character's personality, tastes, values and emotions.

KING EDWARD II

(Scenes 1, 3, 4, 6, 8, 11, 12, 13, 16, 18, 19, 20, 22, 24)
A highly complex character, Edward is not just sybaritic and wastefully irresponsible as the rebels believe him to be. He seems to have lost any secure sense of identity (see Themes, on Loss). For example, he sees Gaveston as himself (see Themes, on Identity). This makes him particularly easily swayed by his friends and advisers, and generally incapable of opposing them in order to do what he feels to be right. A key example is his flight from the battlefield, against his own nobler judgement.

> EDWARD: Give me my horse and let's r'enforce our troops,
> And in this bed of honour die with fame.
> BALDOCK: O no, my lord; this princely resolution
> Fits not the time. Away! We are pursued (Scene 18, lines 6–8).

Frequently Edward is dominated by the emotion of the moment. He is suspicious, almost paranoid, and this pushes him into rash statements and impulsive actions. In particular, a strongly defensive love for his closest friends leads him to offend the hereditary nobility and to deprive the country of the money it needs to prosper. Edward's instability makes him a careless king and a negligent husband. On several occasions love of Gaveston is set up in direct opposition to the King's care for the country. He expresses his disregard for his country at Scene 1, lines 151–2, 'And sooner shall the sea o'erwhelm my land / Than bear the ship that shall transport thee hence' and at Scene 12, lines 30–2, 'Rather than thus be braved, / Make England's civil towns huge heaps of stones / And ploughs to go about our palace gates.'

Through him, the play can analyse the nature of kingship. At first Edward sees kingship as an almost God-like power to change what others see as the natural order. In particular, he believes he has the right to change the social hierarchy and elevate Gaveston: 'Were he a peasant, being my minion, / I'll make the proudest of you stoop to him' (Scene 4, lines 30–1).

Gaveston's new status is staged **symbolically** by seating him next to the King, at an equal level. Gaveston thus briefly takes the place that previously belonged to the Queen, Isabella. Later Edward interprets kingship as courage in battle (Scene 18, lines 5–8 – quoted above), and in military terms, as violent retribution ('If I be King, not one of them shall live' Scene 4, line 105). In both of these Edward's success is short-lived. He fails to see that kingship might imply responsibilities. Geoffrey Bredbeck argues that Edward is caught in the concept of 'the king's two bodies', whereby a monarch was both a physical being with a mortal body, but that there was also a metaphysical kingly body which went on for ever, and which enacted laws, wielded power, held the responsibility of office and was involved in a mystical relationship with the land and the people (see also Marie Axton, *The Queen's Two Bodies*, Royal Hist. Soc., Bondell & Brewer, 1978).

He does at least care about his young son, and worries that young Edward is surrounded by villains.

Let not that Mortimer protect my son,
More safety is there in a tiger's jaws
Than his embracements (Scene 20, lines 115–17).

This strikes us **ironically** as his own closest advisers have repeatedly misjudged the situation to disastrous effect.

Edward's fall is constructed as a sequence of losses, farewells and mourning. As Edward inexorably falls further and further from his exalted position, he comes to a clearer understanding of what he has lost: not just his closest friends and lovers, but his sense of who and what he is. He cared nothing for his position in the opening scenes, but when he comes to give up the crown he sees how important it is to his identity and assumes that abdication is equivalent to death. 'Here, take my crown – the life of Edward too. / Two kings in England cannot reign at once' (Scene 20, lines 57–8).

Even then he does not comprehend how far he was responsible for his own fall: '... Yet how have I transgressed, / Unless it be with too much clemency?' (Scene 20, lines 122–3).

PIERS GAVESTON

(Later referred to as the Earl of Cornwall – Scenes 1, 3, 4, 6, 8, 9, 10)
Edward's close friend and lover, Gaveston in his first speech foreshadows the transgressions against the social hierarchy which he will generate. 'Farewell, base stooping to the lordly peers; / My knee shall bow to none but to the King (Scene 1, lines 18–19).

Gaveston is characterised as tending to support the King's hedonistic impulses by supplying him with luxurious entertainments such as erotic plays, songs and dances (Scene 1, lines 50–70). These are described in exotic, non-English terms ('Italian masques' line 54). Later Gaveston himself is pejoratively described as 'French', and he uses both Italian and French exclamations ('*Tanti!*' line 22, '*Mort Dieu*' line 89). He is a liar, when he pretends that he will help the Three Poor Men (lines 43–5). His attitude towards the Poor Men shows him to be totally lacking in Christian charity and in any sense of willingness to help these poor but deserving Englishmen. He uses **asides**, revealing that he is a dangerous man who utters secret threats ('That villain Mortimer, I'll be his death' – Scene 1, line 80), and indeed is connected with deception more generally via his association with theatricality. His influence is corrupting, when it encourages lies (Scene 1, lines 30–2). Gaveston is totally without tact (or any political caution) when he sneers at ordinary folk ('He nods, and scorns, and smiles at those that pass' – Scene 2, line 24) and vindictively stresses his victory over the nobles (Scene 6, lines 74–8). Nevertheless, he shows absolute loyalty and love towards Edward, and eventually dies for him (Scene 10).

QUEEN ISABELLA

(Wife of Edward II and mother of young Edward – Scenes 2, 4, 6, 8, 11, 15, 17, 18, 21, 23, 25)
Isabella is another major character who changes considerably in the course of the play. Her devotion to her son is the only consistent trait.

QUEEN ISABELLA continued

Marlowe makes her extremely loving and loyal towards Edward at first, distressed because he no longer cares for her and even accuses her of an illicit relationship with Mortimer. Isabella is characterised by weeping and sorrow at this point. She is willing to do almost anything in order to regain Edward's affection, including sharing him with Gaveston. Edward cruelly only likes her as long as she is useful in recalling Gaveston. She is resourceful, however, and instead of meekly suffering this maltreatment (as a proper wife was supposed to do in that period) she leaves for her home, France, seeking support. It is there that the romantic relationship with Mortimer develops, and her tenacity is demonstrated by her presence with the rebel barons when they return to the battlefield in England. Isabella is not a young woman – she has a teenage son – but she is still sexually attractive and politically powerful. She has the intelligence to form plans for her own best advantage, and the courage to carry them through. At the close of the play even her son is willing to suspect her of some part in the murder of his father, but her fate is left unknown as she is courteously led to the Tower.

EDMUND, EARL OF KENT

(Brother to Edward II; frequently referred to as Kent – Scenes 1, 3, 4, 6, 7, 12, 13, 14, 17, 21, 22, 23)
Possibly the most honest and likeable character in the play, Edmund functions by observing and analysing the situation. Edmund is fond of his brother, and begins by being loyal to his cause. When the lords first oppose Edward, Edmund threatens them with execution, thus raising the stakes of the game, and making it clear that their rebellion involves treachery to the King. This inadvertently makes these warrior-nobles even more violent and angry. A rational and moderate thinker, he wisely advises Edward to proceed tactfully, thereby calling down Edward's disapproval. For a time he changes sides, realising that Edward has gone too far and that the country is suffering. He helps Mortimer to escape from the Tower before returning to loyalty to his brother through remorse when he sees how Mortimer is torturing him. Edmund, then, performs the useful function within the play of offering the audience a character with whom they can identify. He makes concrete the dilemma that Edward's character and impossible behaviour pose for reasonable

people: the King is both preposterously tactless, arrogant and foolish, but also in some ways a moral innocent, an **emblem** of the stable social structure, and much to be pitied. Edmund is the only on-stage character to perceive these truths. He becomes yet another in the long list of people who die for Edward, when he attempts to help him escape, and is executed (see Scene 23).

PRINCE EDWARD/EDWARD III

(Scenes 11, 15, 17, 18, 21, 23, 25)
Edward, the son of Edward II and Isabella, is seen as an unequivocally responsible and admirable character as he grows from childhood to adulthood in this tumultuous court. By introducing the character in Scene 11, relatively late in the course of events and after the death of Gaveston, Marlowe avoids some of the stage problems involved in representing a child's gradual maturation through time. He sees his mother's sorrow and accompanies her into exile in France without giving up hope in his father. He perceives his father sympathetically, as an honourable person, and supports his status as king. The Prince refuses to consider himself as a contender for the throne while his father is still alive. As Mortimer's plots proceed, Prince Edward attempts to oppose him and save his uncle Kent from execution. When his authority proves inadequate to this task, he is quick to understand that Mortimer will soon pose a threat to his own life. With political astuteness, he moves to gather the support of the nobles against Mortimer, and ensures that the murder of Edward II is duly punished. He thus demonstrates that he has the qualities required to make a powerful and just king. That position is reinforced by giving him the closing words in the play, and a strong sense of completion results.

SPENCER JUNIOR

(Scenes 5, 6, 8, 11, 12, 13, 16, 18, 19)
Spencer serves the Lady Margaret, Gaveston's fiancée. He meets the King through their mutual friendship with Gaveston, and on Gaveston's death quickly takes his place as Edward's favourite. Beginning with an apparently unscrupulous and money-grubbing attitude, he quickly forms

an affectionate and loyal relationship with the King: a testimony to Edward's ability to inspire love in his followers. The advice he gives as Edward's friend tends to be misjudged – Spencer is out of his depth both socially and politically, but carries this off by swaggering and being assertive. Eventually caught in disguise at the Abbey of Neath, Spencer demonstrates his absolute devotion by being more concerned over losing the King than over his own imminent death. He thus gains a kind of dignity through his disastrous association with Edward.

MORTIMER JUNIOR

(Referred to here as Mortimer – Scenes 1, 2, 4, 6, 7, 8, 9, 12, 13, 14, 15, 17, 18, 21, 23, 25)
Mortimer is abrupt, passionate and fiery, but also devious and increasingly ambitious as the play proceeds. He sees action as noble and silence as 'baseness' (Scene 2, line 27), a position which leads him to express his hatred for Gaveston and so to aggravate the opposition to the King. He is stubborn and strong-willed, implacable in his opposition to Gaveston, and rather eager to move from words to deeds. His guiding intelligence combines with the soldierly mentality of Warwick and Lancaster to speed the play towards military confrontation. Clearly, he should be played as having an attractive, even charismatic personality, for he attracts the affections of the discarded Queen Isabella when she is in exile in France. For someone who cares so much about his position as a noble, it is odd that he eventually descends into ignoble actions such as arranging the maltreatment and murder of the King. This can be explained as a progressive moral decay (see Narrative Structure). It also serves to render Edward II pitiable, and to relocate his position in the scheme of the play – we can begin to forget Edward's follies, and see him as the victim of a fiendish attack, far in excess of his faults. Finally very much the villain of the piece, Mortimer's execution and dismemberment **symbolically** purge the country of its unrest, leaving Edward III a clean slate with which to begin his reign.

Mortimer senior

(Scenes 1, 2, 4)
The uncle of Mortimer junior. For all his frank, assertive speech, he can be a rational, moderate and well-educated man, who gives his nephew good advice. He is in favour of tolerating the King's more flamboyant escapades, on the grounds of the latter's youth. A soldier, he is also concerned about foreign incursions into England, and is taken prisoner in battle against the Scots (see notes on Scene 6).

Guy, earl of warwick

(Referred to as Warwick – Scenes 1, 2, 4, 6, 7, 8, 9, 12, 13)
Warwick is a bluff soldier, clearly older than Edward II, since he is described as white-haired, and his primary loyalty is to the instructions of the dead King Edward I. He is easily enraged, and will not stand to be contradicted or threatened. His dynamism is expressed by his speedy entrances, and exits accompanied by 'Away' as the only word in a line. There is something of the classic cinematic villain (one imagines Darth Vader from *Star Wars*) in his sweeping, dominant style. For all his noble title, it is Warwick who breaks his word and has Gaveston executed with no opportunity to say farewell to the King (Scene 10). He is executed in his turn for his part in the first rebellion (Scene 13).

Lancaster

(Scenes 1, 2, 4, 6, 7, 8, 9, 12, 13)
One of the nobles who oppose Edward II and Gaveston, and a powerful leader of the rebellious armies. He is a soldier, and the issues he cares about are to do with paying his soldiers. He and Gaveston have a strong antipathy to each other, but he is not directly instrumental in Gaveston's hasty death (Scene 9). Nevertheless, Edward has Lancaster executed in the aftermath (Scene 13).

MINOR CHARACTERS

BISHOP OF COVENTRY

(*Scene 2*) He is present as a stage **emblem**: evidence of Edward's anger and refusal to bow to any traditional authority of rules or social expectations. He shows Edward's disregard for anything sacred including the Church, in comparison with his regard for Gaveston. Like Warwick, Coventry was instrumental in having Gaveston banished during Edward I's reign, before the beginning of the play, and Edward's response in wanting to hurt those who have hurt him is childish, politically impractical and unChristian. It is especially shocking that Edward should attack and humiliate a priest, and this immediately turns the whole Church against him. An Elizabethan audience, however, may well have found this insult to a Catholic prelate hilarious.

BISHOP OF CANTERBURY

(*Scenes 2, 4*) The Bishop joins with the nobles in petitioning for Gaveston's exile. His presence adds numbers to the crowd opposed to Edward. On stage his clerical robes would make it clear that he symbolically adds a second social group – the clergy – to the nobles who already oppose Edward and his friends. This shows how quickly and thoroughly Edward's behaviour alienates him from his world, and how little he cares about it (see Themes).

PEMBROKE AND BEAUMONT

(*Scene 4*) Pembroke is a rebel noble who serves to swell the stage presence of the numbers who disapprove of Edward's behaviour. Beaumont recalls Gaveston from exile.

BALDOCK

(*Scenes 5, 6, 11, 13, 18, 19*) Having been tutor to the Lady Margaret, Baldock moves to court as an associate of Spencer's. He describes himself as deceitful: precise in appearance, but inwardly immoral ('apt for any kind of villainy' – Scene 5, line 51). His social station means that he is probably poor, and will have to depend on being useful to wealthier patrons in order to make a living. Choosing the dissolute Gaveston shows him to be easily corruptible.

LADY MARGARET DE CLARE

(*Scenes 5, 6, 8*) Daughter of the late Earl of Gloucester, Lady Margaret is engaged to be married to Gaveston, whom she appears to love sincerely. In her behaviour she is the model of the dutiful wife.

MALTRAVERS

(*Scenes 9, 11, 16, 21, 22*) Wiggins & Lindsey argue, in my opinion wrongly, that Maltravers and ARUNDEL are the same person throughout the play, and use the speech-heading 'Maltravers' for all speeches by either. Forker uses Arundel for all the speeches in Scenes 9, 11 and 16 and reserves 'Matrevis' for the character in Scenes 21 and 22. In Scene 9, Maltravers (Arundel) is one of the lords loyal to Edward II and acts as a messenger between him and the barons, carrying reports accurately. He has the courage and grace to offer himself as a hostage in Gaveston's place, and is highly thought of by both parties. Mortimer says of him: 'we know thou art a noble gentleman' (Scene 9, line 68). By Scene 21, the character called 'Maltravers' or 'Matrevis' is working for Mortimer as a messenger. He is prepared to behave unkindly towards Edward and agrees to Mortimer's command to 'amplify his grief with bitter words' (line 64). He follows this up by brutally shaving Edward with puddle water (Scene 22, lines 27–33), and taking Kent prisoner in the course of his rescue attempt. This unexplained disjunction in the character's behaviour suggests strongly that two different people are intended. If it is the same person, then we see a character who betrays Edward and goes over to Mortimer's side, perhaps making the suffering of the King even more poignant, since it is at the hands of someone he has trusted.

SIR JOHN OF HAINAULT

(*Scenes 15, 17*) Sir John courteously offers Isabella assistance when her brother, the King of France, has refused to help her. He provides loyalty and encouragement, not to mention a venue where she can liaise with Mortimer and collect an army to attack Edward.

RHYS AP HOWELL

(*Scenes 18, 19*) As a Welshman who takes Mortimer's side, Rhys's presence shows that opposition to Edward has spread through the entire kingdom. He represents the citizens of Bristol. He is more than willing to be involved in the capture of the King and his followers.

MAYOR OF BRISTOL
(*Scene 18*) A representative of a far-flung region of the country, but also of the middling classes of the populace. A mayor was often a rather well-to-do merchant, and not of the nobility. With him, we see that honest, ordinary people have now turned against Edward.

ABBOT OF NEATH
(*Scene 19*) Here we have a Churchman who holds no grudge against Edward, and seeks to protect him in a truly Christian manner. The honest Abbot promises absolute secrecy. It is **ironic** that Edward's first outrageous act was against the Church, and now his last haven is with an abbot. Here, Edward can see that a quiet life has many advantages.

MOWER
(*Scene 19*) One of the most striking minor characters, the Mower is both a simple labourer in the fields, and an **allegorical** image of Death. He is a dark-looking person, carrying a kind of scythe called a Welsh hook. His job of mowing the field reminds one of the Old Testament: 'All flesh is grass' (Isaiah, 40:6). Some have objected that the stage **emblem** of death is a little obvious, but one could argue that his presence fits into the broad canvas of social stations that appears on the stage in the course of this play.

LEICESTER
(*Scenes 19, 20*) Leicester is one of the few opponents of Edward to show him any common humanity or respect, which he achieves even while functioning as Edward's gaoler. It is at Leicester's castle of Kenilworth (sometimes called 'Killingworth' in early editions) that Edward is first imprisoned.

BISHOP OF WINCHESTER
(*Scene 20*) This bishop is brought on to accept Edward's crown. It is appropriate that a churchman should be present for the uncrowning, as

the original coronation ceremony is also a religious one. Winchester's
presence thus tends to legitimate the action.

TRUSSEL

(*Scene 20*) Trussel is apparently a representative of Parliament, and thus
probably belongs to the middle classes or gentry. Like Winchester's, his
presence at the uncrowning adds legitimacy: a sense of official authority.

BERKELEY

(*Scene 20*) The Earl of Berkeley, another of the barons who follow
Mortimer, provides a harsher imprisonment than Leicester does. His
home, Berkeley Castle, is the location of Edward's murder.

GOURNEY

(*Scenes 21, 22*) In social class, Gourney is a trusted servant of Mortimer.
In behaviour, he becomes degraded into a gaoler to Edward, and one of
his tormentors, though he stops short of actual torture. His specialities
are mental cruelty, and setting up situations which the King will find
physically deeply uncomfortable and humiliating.

LIGHTBORNE

(Scenes 23, 24) The murderer Lightborne is characterised as
knowledgeable about sinister foreign methods of murder. He is famous
for knowing several ways to kill a person and leave no trace, and his
skills are easily bought. Thus, if Edward's exoticism was his major
pleasure, it is **ironically** appropriate that a comparable exoticism
concludes his downfall. Many commentators have noticed the similarity
between his name and Lucifer: the angel who became the chief devil in
hell. It adds to the sense that Edward is in hell – he may have been there
all along, and is now simply descending to an even deeper pit. Lightborne
speaks to Edward almost kindly, offering him sympathy and soothing
words, and so catching him off guard when he wants Edward held down
to perform the murder.

CHAMPION

(*Scene 23*) This is an official anonymous figure who is part of the
ceremony of Edward III's coronation. It is a peculiar moment, as he is

clearly simply a ceremonial figure. His asserted function of fighting traitors is not invoked when Kent is brought on stage accused of precisely that crime. He is therefore a 'show', similar in some ways to the plays that Edward II indulged in when he was in power. One might interpret him, then, as a resurgence of the old habits, or as a sign that acting is necessary to state power. Perhaps one should see this figure as a show which deals with the acceptable topics of politics and warfare, rather than the less acceptable topic of eroticism.

THE THREE POOR MEN

(*Scene 1*) These three characters represent the poor English peasantry, part of the stations of English life (see Themes, on England, and Textual Analysis, Text 1). They introduce the theme of class relations and of the duties one class of society owes to another, which will reappear throughout the play. They are not beggars as they offer to work for their keep, but they do depend on employment or patronage to live. Each represents a different kind of merit. One is potentially useful since he can ride; the second has experience from having travelled; and the third deserves gratitude for having served his country. Gaveston rejects their merits and values the traveller only in so far as he can tell entertaining lies.

OTHER MINOR CHARACTERS

The Clerk of the Crown (*Scene 4*), Post (*Scenes 6, 16*), Guard (*Scene 6*), James (*Scene 9*), Horse Boy (*Scene 9*) and the Monks (*Scene 19*) display the involvement of other social classes in events: the row between Edward and his nobles affects many people besides themselves.

NARRATIVE STRUCTURE

In *From 'Mankind' to Marlowe* (Harvard, 1962) David Bevington talks about the kind of fluid staging that Marlowe uses to bring characters on and off stage in such a way that the action keeps going with as little break as possible. This provides a sense of great pace, and contributes to the skill with which Marlowe compresses the events of twenty years into a single dynamic narrative sweep. The speed of Marlowe's version makes Edward's fall seem inevitable, and runs rapidly over the more successful aspects of the historical reign. To some extent the apparent structure of *Edward II* in twenty-five discrete scenes has been imposed on it by editors. Some believe that five Acts can be detected, and many editions (such as the Penguin *Complete Works of Christopher Marlowe* and the Revels Plays edition) are divided into Acts and scenes. This kind of formal structure is helpful for identifying portions of text, but there are also complex narrative patterns in *Edward II* which function to relate scenes to one another. In the Synopsis I mentioned the narrative movements into which the play can be divided. Several possible views exist:

- the **tragedy** of the gradual decline of a great man into downfall: thus, the loss of the possibility of greatness through a tragic flaw, in this case pride. Clifford Leech, in his *Tragedy* (Critical Idiom Series, Routledge, 1990) elaborates on this classical structure. Such a description sees the play as essentially a single movement: Edward's trajectory towards death.
- the two-part movement in which (first) Edward's relationship with Gaveston leads to the estrangement of the barons and of his wife, Isabella. For much of the first movement, some possibilities of reconciliation are held out. This is followed by the second, darker movement, where his political misjudgements and his attachment to the Spencers lead him into less and less honourable courses. His wife deserts him for an adulterous liaison with Mortimer, and together with the barons, the opposition to Edward becomes more implacable and unscrupulous. In this way, the two parts of the fall of Edward are matched by the gradual rise to power of Mortimer. Mortimer also falls, of course, with great rapidity, at the close of the play. This reading can make much use of the 'wheel of Fortune' image, in which a rise must inevitably be followed by a fall (and vice versa).
- one might see a single structure here too: the gradual corruption of morals within a country when it is badly governed, since both Edward and the barons adopt more and more dishonourable practices, including cowardice and murder. This theme of the moral importance of good government was strong in the Early Modern period.

One of Marlowe's narrative techniques is to foreshadow events through curses or promises. Gaveston's opening speech envisages the entertainments that he will provide for Edward, and we are later told how much the barons object to these. Edward's curse on Mortimer comes true:

> This poor revenge hath something eased my mind.
> So may his limbs be torn, as is this paper!
> Hear me, immortal Jove, and grant it too (Scene 20 lines 141–3).

Intriguingly, however, there are also predictions that do not come true: Isabella's fear that her son will not live for long is not answered within the play, but all who saw it would know that Edward III reigned long and successfully (1327–77). 'Ah, boy, this towardness makes thy mother fear / Thou art not marked to many days on earth' (Scene 11, lines 79–80).

Mortimer's prophetic curse in Scene 18, asking that Edward's voyage to Ireland should be turned back by storms, comes uncannily true, but serves the banal narrative function of preparing the audience to comprehend the situation when precisely this has happened in Scene 19. Curses that come true give a play a sense of inevitability, and in a way this is so, since the audience knows that certain historical events happened, and the play must work with those. Thus, the sense of premonition is entirely appropriate to a **history play**.

The theme of gutters and water, of 'low' versions of more dignified ceremonies begins in Scene 1 and carries through to the death of the King. Edward himself begins it with the retributive assault on the Bishop of Coventry: 'And in the channel christen him anew' (Scene 1, line 187). This foreshadows other events: the execution of Gaveston in a ditch (reported by Maltravers at Scene 11, lines 115–20), the forcible shaving of Edward in a gutter (Scene 22, lines 27–32) and the incarceration of Edward in the cess-pit of Kenilworth Castle (Scene 24). A second water theme concerns the sea. To be on the sea or abroad is to be temporarily both safe and outside England. Characters' fates change markedly when they take to the water. Where puddle water involves inversion, the sea also involves a change of fortunes.

STAGING

Originally, this play was probably designed for a Shakespearean type of stage, with a large 'thrust stage' projecting into the open-air auditorium in such a way that the members of the audience could be very close to the action, and feel involved in it and with one another. Such stages are described in detail in Glynne Wickham, *Early English Stages*, vol. 2, part 2 (Routledge, 1972). The Globe, a full-size replica of a Shakespearean theatre from the 1590s, and very like the acting space on which *Edward II* would have appeared, has been constructed on London's South Bank. Students who are interested in theatre history might well pay it a visit.

Other venues may have been civic halls and the halls or courtyards of inns, all of which are known to have been used for theatrical performances in the latter part of the sixteenth century. Most of these locations tend to create an informal, spontaneous atmosphere with the audience positioned close to the players. For a modern equivalent, a **theatre-in-the-round** or a pub theatre would be very appropriate. Few props are required, and indeed a highly elaborate or realistic stage set would be undesirable, slowing down the action and the transitions between scenes. For further discussion of production issues, see also the various discussions in Characterisation (above) for thoughts about interpreting roles.

Marlowe uses a strikingly flexible stage, with few or no props. Scene 18 is a good example, showing how the stage can, in rapid succession, represent a battlefield, a location where Kent can be alone; next, and within the same scene, it represents a location where the Court, including Isabella and the child Prince Edward can arrive and discuss matters. Immediately then it becomes a place to which Rhys ap Howell can bring Spencer senior in captivity. Thus it is a **symbolic** battlefield, where staging functions on a superbly surreal level, and where realism is not just unnecessary but undesirable. It is, in psychoanalytic terms, a location where the unconscious mind can have free play.

This kind of flexibility clearly poses problems for any sort of **conventional** or realistic staging, and *Edward II* works best in a minimalist setting, where costumes and hand-held props carry the weight of signification. The rapid changes from one area of England to another might be signified by the use of regional accents, an approach suggested by the presence of local people in various scenes (the Mower at Neath; the Mayor of Bristol for example). The medium best suited to a realistic setting with rapid changes of scene is of course the cinema. Such techniques as the rapid intercutting of scenes showing the pursued and the pursuers are ideal for *Edward II*. One can imagine a thoroughly gory and seamless production in the manner of the action movie, a mode which notoriously cuts from one location to another with great energy.

LANGUAGE

By virtue of Marlowe's mastery, the **iambic pentameter** line in **blank verse** became the standard metre of Elizabethan and Jacobean drama. Marlowe did not invent this structure, but adapted it from Chaucer's rhymed iambic pentameter poetry and from Robert Peele's experiments with blank verse on the stage. In *Tamburlaine* Marlowe used a blank verse line whose rhythm was accurate and precise. Once this basic five-stress regularity was established, variations on its structure could be made. Marlowe's subsequent writing begins that process of reiteration, syncopation and variation which in the next decade was ramified by Shakespeare into a flexible run-on line. The English language had reached a point of development where it offered dramatists and poets a combination of simplicity and variety, clarity and flexibility in the **syntax** and a vocabulary which was rapidly becoming more and more enriched. Marlowe's diction profited from this richness, adding to it a sense of speed through the bold use of **polysyllables**, and resonance with proper names. ('Gaveston' and 'Isabella' are good examples: polysyllabic proper names which suit Marlowe's poetic style impeccably.) Whenever the two join forces at the end of a line the effect is especially strong. An example of this kind of 'poetry of excess' is the extraordinarily powerful effect achieved by repetition of that final polysyllabic proper name. Scene 4, lines 287–334 contain an insistent repetition of 'Gaveston': six times at the ends of lines and three further occurrences mid-line. That name is intertwined in a dance-like sequence with 'Isabel' (three times) 'Mortimer' (twice), 'Lancaster', 'Pembroke' and 'Edward' (once each). Litanies of names like this recur throughout the play.

Mythological and geographical reverberations add to the impressive qualities of the Marlovian line. The Furies, the Fates, Jove and Ganymede and many others populate the linguistic and imaginative world, as do Caucasus, Elysium and the many English place names. For all this fantasy, language is remarkably direct. Simple statements and direct instructions predominate mingled with the simple adjective + noun of address or abuse ('vile torpedo'; 'sweet Mortimer' and so on). The resulting energy is controlled by the sense of the line as a complete unit. Marlowe avoids **enjambment** (runovers) by concluding sentences or phrases at the ends of lines. The lines are then built into larger structures of discourse, which one might call verse-sentences, or verse-paragraphs.

Marlowe's **diction** is characterised by his use of superlatives and of extreme or **hyperbolic** language, while his **imagery** involves the use of verbs which have a spatial quality such as 'surmounts', 'soaring', but also 'stoop' and 'droop'. This is especially striking in Edward's concerns about the rebellious lords, and fits with images of the social hierarchy as depth and height, and of the Wheel of Fortune.

This section relies heavily on Harry Levin, *Christopher Marlowe: The Overreacher* (Faber & Faber, 1961) and its description of Marlowe's verse and language, pages 28–31 and 41.

PART FOUR

TEXTUAL ANALYSIS

TEXT 1 (SCENE 1 LINES 24–96)

Gaveston has just arrived back in England from exile. His personality is
revealed through his encounter with the Three Poor Men. With graphic
economy the scene then displays the origins and nature of the dispute on
which Edward's reign will founder, and the violently antipathetic
personalities involved.

GAVESTON
But how now, what are these?

POOR MEN
Such as desire your worship's service.   25

GAVESTON
What canst thou do?

FIRST POOR MAN
I can ride.

GAVESTON
But I have no horses. What art thou?

SECOND POOR MAN
A traveller.

GAVESTON
Let me see, thou wouldst do well to wait at my trencher   30
and tell me lies at dinner-time; and, as I like your dis-
coursing, I'll have you. And what art thou?

THIRD POOR MAN
A soldier, that hath served against the Scot.

GAVESTON
Why, there are hospitals for such as you;
I have no war, and therefore, sir, be gone.   35

THIRD POOR MAN
Farewell, and perish by a soldier's hand,
That wouldst reward them with an hospital.

GAVESTON

[*Aside*] Ay, ay. These words of his move me as much
As if a goose should play the porcupine,
And dart her plumes, thinking to pierce my breast.   40
But yet it is no pain to speak men fair;
I'll flatter these and make them live in hope.
[*To them*] You know that I came lately out of France,
And yet I have not viewed my lord the King;
If I speed well, I'll entertain you all.   45

POOR MEN

We thank your worship.

GAVESTON

I have some business; leave me to myself.

POOR MEN

We will wait here about the court.   *Exeunt*

GAVESTON

Do. These are not men for me;
I must have wanton poets, pleasant wits,   50
Musicians, that with touching of a string
May draw the pliant King which way I please.
Music and poetry is his delight;
Therefore I'll have Italian masques by night,
Sweet speeches, comedies, and pleasing shows;   55
And in the day when he shall walk abroad,
Like sylvan nymphs my pages shall be clad,
My men like satyrs grazing on the lawns
Shall with their goat-feet dance an antic hay;
Sometime a lovely boy in Dian's shape,   60
With hair that gilds the water as it glides,
Crownets of pearl about his naked arms,
And in his sportful hands an olive tree
To hide those parts which men delight to see,
Shall bathe him in a spring; and there hard by,   65
One like Actaeon peeping through the grove,
Shall by the angry goddess be transformed,

And running in the likeness of an hart,
By yelping hounds pulled down, and seem to die.
Such things as these best please his majesty.   70

Enter [EDWARD] *the King,* LANCASTER, MORTIMER SENIOR, MORTIMER JUNIOR,
EDMUND EARL OF KENT, GUY EARL OF WARWICK *[and attendants]*

My lord! Here comes the King and the nobles
From the parliament; I'll stand aside.

EDWARD
Lancaster.

LANCASTER
My lord.

GAVESTON
[Aside] That Earl of Lancaster do I abhor.   75

EDWARD
Will you not grant me this? *[Aside]* In spite of them
I'll have my will, and these two Mortimers
That cross me thus shall know I am displeased.

MORTIMER SENIOR
If you love us, my lord, hate Gaveston.

GAVESTON
[Aside] That villain Mortimer, I'll be his death.   80

MORTIMER JUNIOR
Mine uncle here, this earl, and I myself
Were sworn to your father at his death,
That he should ne'er return into the realm;
And know, my lord, ere I will break my oath,
This sword of mine, that should offend your foes,   85
Shall sleep within the scabbard at thy need,
And underneath thy banners march who will,
For Mortimer will hang his armour up.

GAVESTON
[Aside] Mort Dieu!

EDWARD

Well Mortimer, I'll make thee rue these words.   90
Beseems it thee to contradict thy King?
Frownst thou thereat, aspiring Lancaster?
The sword shall plane the furrows of thy brows
And hew these knees that now are grown so stiff.
I will have Gaveston; and you shall know   95
What danger 'tis to stand against your King.

Gaveston is visibly present on stage throughout, with considerable
dramatic effect. His centrality to the plot is stated by his place in the
opening scene. It follows an opening twenty-four lines spoken by
Gaveston alone on the stage, creating a satisfying artistic sequence: one
speaker; a small group of four speakers together; one speaker alone again;
a much larger group in a state of high emotion; and lastly, after the
end of the excerpt, a bringing together of all the characters so far.

The excerpt covers two separate kinds of event: Gaveston's
unselfconscious response to the Three Poor Men, followed by his secret
observation of the barons and King. We thus see Gaveston when he is
unobserved and the barons when they think they are unobserved by
Gaveston. Both structures give Gaveston great power: we see him
behaving badly to the Three Poor Men, and we see him gaining the
power of a secret knowledge of the barons' opinions. Before this excerpt
begins, Gaveston has been alone on stage (a very dominant situation)
envisaging his future with the King. The Three Poor Men are
anonymous, which gives them an **archetypal**, or even **allegorical** quality.
They stand for poverty within England. In a few lines of conversation
they expose Gaveston's selfishness and enact in miniature the neglect of
the kingdom and the people that will later antagonise the barons against
him and Edward. Though not strictly a **dumb show**, this exchange
performs some of the functions of one. The exchange with Gaveston has a
ritual, catechistic quality as each Poor Man is asked a question, responds
and is dismissed. The exchange is conducted in prose rather than verse,
which makes it sound informal or off-hand. By asking Gaveston for work
the Three Poor Men invoke the conventions of the feudal and Early
Modern class structure, whereby poor people made a living by serving a
master, who supported them with upkeep, clothing and gifts. The phrase

'masterless man' then was similar to the concept 'homeless' now. These are not beggars, then, but people legitimately trying to insert themselves into the social structure. Gaveston demonstrates that he belongs outside conventional social structures by rejecting them. Gaveston addresses each as 'thou' – a familiar form of 'you' used towards inferiors, animals and children, but also for intimate friends. Although they have no names, the three represent three different kinds of claim to usefulness. The horseman is clearly of practical use, and his profession may suggest a rural background. The traveller is more dubious: he has presumably been abroad, and so is experienced, but has no way of earning a living. Tainted with foreignness, he is perceived as a potential liar (see Themes, on England). His situation could become desperate. Gaveston implies that the traveller might be of some use to tell entertaining lies, thereby both insulting him and giving him false hope, for he does not intend to employ any of them. The third man has earned gratitude because he has served his country in the army. In suggesting a hospital, Gaveston is condemning him to eke out his life on meagre and humiliating charity. Angered, the soldier utters the first of the prophetic curses in the play (see Narrative Technique). Gaveston will indeed 'perish by a soldier's hand' (line 36) when the Earl of Warwick hacks his head off (as reported in Scene 11). In brushing off the curse, Gaveston manifests his ingrained inability to listen to opposition.

   Gaveston is probably now on stage alone again. It would be possible to keep the Three Poor Men on, as they say they will remain 'about the court'. Their presence would help to swell the courtly crowd scene which will shortly follow. Before that, however, comes Gaveston's famous monologue. This is not heard by other characters, but it is now generally agreed that **soliloquies** such as this should be played as the character confiding in the audience. Shared knowledge creates an intimacy between Gaveston and the audience. Also typical of the soliloquy form, Gaveston enunciates his plans about the future. He intends to hold sway over the King, whom he sees as 'pliant' (line 52), by keeping him entertained by a series of sophisticated, even decadent performances. There will be a wide range of these, crossing the boundaries between pretence and reality. The 'wanton poets' and 'pleasant wits' are real people as are the musicians. They are to produce charming works of art. The phrase 'Italian masques' reveals that the evening entertainments will involve theatrical pretence, though never of a serious or **tragic** nature. Italy here is seen as a source of sophistication and learning, but there is also an implied hint of corruption. This Italianate knowledge of the theatrical both masks and foreshadows the sinister Italian knowledge of violent murder used by Lightborne in Scene 24 to kill Edward. The play consistently presents a connection with foreignness as destructive of Englishness (see Themes, on England). Gaveston goes on to imagine a blurring of reality and fantasy. No longer confined to their accepted location, tableaux and presentations will pop up around Edward as if they were real, in the course of his ordinary daily life. Edward's grip on reality is none too strong, and Gaveston's plans will loosen it further (see Themes, on Identity).

All the scenes imagined by Gaveston involve eroticism and often gender-confusion. Boys will be dressed as nymphs or as the Greek goddess Diana, men will dance as satyrs (a mythical half-goat creature, notorious for their sexual endowments). Servants chosen for their beauty will also act out scenes from classical mythology with false modesty. The semi-naked décor serves only to draw attention to those parts which are scarcely hidden. The story of Actaeon, for example, could be seen as an eroticising of violent death, similar to the pleasure the audience may later derive from viewing Edward's death. It causes us to ask ourselves very modern questions about the pleasures of violent theatre. As Gaveston narrates these sights, he draws us into the enchanted world of his own imagination. The **diction** is lushly descriptive, filled with adjectival clauses ('that gilds the water') and phrases ('crownets of pearl about his naked arms') and reminders of theatricality ('*like* Actaeon'; 'in *likeness* of an hart'; '*seem* to die' – my italic).

Gaveston's diction is vastly different from the abrupt phrases of the lords, and even from Edward's habitual logical speech modes. His style most resembles Isabella's syntactically complex speech in Scene 4, lines 170–86, or the plaintive tones Edward uses in captivity in Scene 22. Its sensuality also resembles the mode of the narrative poems such as Marlowe's *Hero and Leander*.

When Edward and the lords appear, Gaveston fades into the background, but retains the audience's awareness of his presence by commenting on what he overhears. We thus hear how deeply he hates the lords and they him. There is clearly something surreptitious and

devious about his concealment at this point, which begins to structure the
audience's attitude to this otherwise charismatic character. The language
of the lords' exchange with Edward is more typical of the play as a whole,
involving abrupt insults and commands which raise the emotional
temperature on both sides. Violence is soon offered in a series of rapidly
escalating threats.

Within this first scene, Marlowe has offered us a rich diversity of
dramatic modes: the use of a letter to convey information; the monologue
or soliloquy; **emblematic** representation or **allegory** (in the Poor Men); a
description of theatre; a secret observer of action; and an impressive
crowd scene where feelings run high.

TEXT 2   (SCENE 11, LINES 89–147)

In this scene, very close to the centre of the play, Edward and the
audience hear a detailed report of Gaveston's death. It is a pivotal
moment, at the close of the first 'movement' (see Narrative Structure). In
the lines immediately prior to the extract, Spencer has clearly begun to
take Gaveston's place as friend and adviser to the King, and in this way
the beginning of the second 'movement' is woven into the close of the
first.

Enter LORD MALTRAVERS

EDWARD
What, Lord Maltravers, dost thou come alone?

MALTRAVERS
Yea, my good lord, for Gaveston is dead.   90

EDWARD
Ah, traitors, have they put my friend to death?
Tell me, Maltravers, died he ere thou cam'st,
Or didst thou see my friend to take his death?

MALTRAVERS
Neither, my lord, for as he was surprised,
Begirt with weapons and with enemies round,   95
I did your highness' message to them all,
Demanding him of them – entreating rather –

And said, upon the honour of my name,
That I would undertake to carry him
Unto your highness, and to bring him back.   100

EDWARD
And tell me, would the rebels deny me that?

SPENCER JUNIOR
Proud recreants!

EDWARD
                    Yea, Spencer, traitors all.

MALTRAVERS
I found them at the first inexorable;
The Earl of Warwick would not bide the hearing,
Mortimer hardly; Pembroke and Lancaster   105
Spake least. And when they flatly had denied,
Refusing to receive me pledge for him,
The Earl of Pembroke mildly thus bespake:
'My lords, because our sovereign sends for him
And promiseth he shall be safe returned,   110
I will this undertake: to have him hence
And see him re-delivered to your hands.'

EDWARD
Well, and how fortunes that he came not?

SPENCER JUNIOR
Some treason or some villainy was cause.

MALTRAVERS
The Earl of Warwick seized him on his way,   115
For, being delivered unto Pembroke's men,
Their lord rode home, thinking his prisoner safe;
But ere he came, Warwick in ambush lay,
And bare him to his death, and in a trench
Struck off his head, and marched unto the camp.   120

SPENCER JUNIOR
A bloody part, flatly against law of arms.

EDWARD
O, shall I speak, or shall I sigh and die?

SPENCER JUNIOR
My lord, refer your vengeance to the sword
Upon these barons; hearten up your men.
Let them not unrevenged murder your friends.   125
Advance your standard, Edward, in the field,
And march to fire them from their starting holes.

EDWARD
[*Kneeling*] By earth, the common mother of us all,
By heaven and all the moving orbs thereof,
By this right hand and by my father's sword,   130
And all the honours 'longing to my crown,
I will have heads and lives for him as many
As I have manors, castles, towns, and towers.
Treacherous Warwick! Traitorous Mortimer!
If I be England's king, in lakes of gore   135
Your headless trunks, your bodies will I trail,
That you may drink your fill and quaff in blood,
And stain my royal standard with the same,
That so my bloody colours may suggest
Remembrance of revenge immortally   140
On your accursèd traitorous progeny –
You villains that have slain my Gaveston.
And in this place of honour and of trust,
Spencer, sweet Spencer, I adopt thee here;
And merely of our love we do create thee   145
Earl of Gloucester and Lord Chamberlain,
Despite of times, despite of enemies.

Lord Maltravers, Earl of Arundel (see Characterisation) makes a report
which is clear, honest and accurate. We know this to be so as we have
already seen most of his report enacted in Scene 10, with the exception
of the actual death. The division of the narrative method between Scenes
10 and 11 is thus a division between representation and recounting,
displaying two ways in which the stage can deal with historical events.

The technique also speeds the action by overlapping Edward's reaction to the news with the audience's first knowledge of the full details. Maltravers's report has a dignified, grave quality, reminiscent of epic poetry, and Edward's questions are equally direct.

It is Spencer who reacts most violently at first, and who urges Edward to take violent retribution against the barons. Where Edward is rational ('Well, and how fortunes that he came not?' line 113), Spencer is inflammatory ('Some treason or some villainy was cause' line 114). Edward's first reaction is very different, even introverted – 'O shall I speak or shall I sigh and die?' (line 122) – focusing on himself rather than on Gaveston or the barons. To respond with a divided set of options, couched as a question, shows Edward as enfeebled.

Into that indecisive space, Spencer's advice falls persuasively. It would be clear to a contemporary audience that Spencer has undue influence over Edward. The King should listen to a group of experienced councillors, not to one young friend, before taking decisions of national importance. Listening to bad advice was a familiar contributing factor to the falls of princes in traditional stories (see Literary Background, on The *de casibus* Tradition).

Edward's solemn oath promises a violent revenge, far in excess of any reasonable response. Maltravers has made it clear that the Earl of Warwick alone was responsible for Gaveston's death. Edward envisages his revenge in terms of the geography of his kingdom (see Themes, on England), but it is scarcely just or admirable to threaten so many deaths. Indeed, he almost seems to usurp the role of an Old Testament God when he condemns his enemies' descendants as traitors for ever (lines 140–1).

Here, though, we see a side of Edward which is uttered in dignified, majestic tones. As poetry, his speech is impressive. He swears by a range of sacred icons: heaven and earth, his own kingship and humanity and his father's power. Its length and coherence contrast with the brief speeches before it and Marlowe creates flowing continuity by interspersing **enjambment** with his more habitual **end-stopped** lines (see Reading *Edward II*). Four examples of enjambment can be readily located:

- 'as many / As I have manors' (lines 132–3)
- 'in lakes of gore / Your headless trunks, your bodies will I trail' (lines 135–6)

- 'may suggest / Remembrance of revenge immortally / On your accursèd traitorous progeny' (lines 139–41)

Edward's passion pounds out in the two four-stress lines which vary the smoothness of the regular **iambic pentameter**. 'Treach'erous War'wick! Trait'orous Mort'imer!' (line 134) and 'Despite' of times', despite' of en'emies' (line 147). These lines have a strong **caesura**, making them even more emphatic. When the actor Simon Russell Beale describes the role of Edward II as 'sheer concentrated self-flagellation' (quoted in the Introduction to the New Mermaids edition, p. xx) it is this verbal habit of intense, unceasing passion to which he refers.

Finally, Edward turns to Spencer, reiterating his name in loving terms, and bestows Gaveston's titles upon him. He thus hastily selects his next favourite, and flings down to the lords the identical provocation that caused them to kill Gaveston.

TEXT 3   (SCENE 23, LINES 1–70)

The close of the play focuses on Edward's gradual degradation and death. Parallel with that is Mortimer's much more sudden from the heights of power to summary execution. This scene reveals Mortimer's moral decay. He is clearly unfit to govern the country.

Enter MORTIMER [JUNIOR] *alone*

MORTIMER JUNIOR

The King must die, or Mortimer goes down;

The commons now begin to pity him.

Yet he that is the cause of Edward's death

Is sure to pay for it when his son is of age,

And therefore will I do it cunningly.   5

This letter, written by a friend of ours,

Contains his death, yet bids them save his life:

[*He reads*] '*Edwardum occidere nolite timere, bonum est*;

Fear not to kill the King, 'tis good he die.'

But read it thus, and that's another sense: 10

'*Edwardum occidere nolite, timere bonum est*;

Kill not the King, 'tis good to fear the worst.'

Unpointed as it is, thus shall it go,
That, being dead, if it chance to be found,
Maltravers and the rest may bear the blame,   15
And we be quit that caused it to be done.
Within this room is locked the messenger
That shall convey it and perform the rest.
And by a secret token that he bears,
Shall he be murdered when the deed is done.   20
Lightborne, come forth.

[Enter LIGHTBORNE*]*
                    Art thou as resolute as thou wast?

LIGHTBORNE
What else, my lord? And far more resolute.

MORTIMER JUNIOR
And hast thou cast how to accomplish it?

LIGHTBORNE
Ay, ay, and none shall know which way he died.

MORTIMER JUNIOR
But at his looks, Lightborne, thou wilt relent.   25

LIGHTBORNE
Relent? Ha, ha! I use much to relent.

MORTIMER JUNIOR
Well, do it bravely, and be secret.

LIGHTBORNE
You shall not need to give instructions;
'Tis not the first time I have killed a man.
I learned in Naples how to poison flowers,   30
To strangle with a lawn thrust through the throat,
To pierce the windpipe with a needle's point,
Or, whilst one is asleep, to take a quill
And blow a little powder in his ears,
Or open his mouth and pour quicksilver down.   35
But yet I have a braver way than these.

MORTIMER JUNIOR
What's that?

LIGHTBORNE
Nay, you shall pardon me; none shall know my tricks.

MORTIMER JUNIOR
I care not how it is, so it be not spied.
Deliver this to Gourney and Maltravers.   40
[*He gives the letter to* LIGHTBORNE]
At every ten miles' end thou hast a horse.
[*Giving a token*] Take this. Away, and never see me more.

LIGHTBORNE
No?

MORTIMER JUNIOR
No, unless thou bring me news of Edward's death.

LIGHTBORNE
That will I quickly do. Farewell, my lord.   45

                    [*Exit*]

MORTIMER JUNIOR
The Prince I rule, the Queen do I command,
And with a lowly congé to the ground
The proudest lords salute me as I pass;
I seal, I cancel, I do what I will.
Feared am I more than loved; let me be feared,   50
And when I frown, make all the court look pale.
I view the Prince with Aristarchus' eyes,
Whose looks were as a breeching to a boy.
They thrust upon me the protectorship
And sue to me for that that I desire.   55
While at the council table, grave enough,
And not unlike a bashful Puritan,
First I complain of imbecility,
Saying it is *onus quam gravissimum*,
Till being interrupted by my friends,   60

Suscepi that *provinciam*, as they term it,
And to conclude, I am Protector now.
Now all is sure: the Queen and Mortimer
Shall rule the realm, the King, and none rule us.
Mine enemies will I plague, my friends advance,   65
And what I list command, who dare control?
Maior sum quam cui possit fortuna nocere.
And that this be the coronation day,
It pleaseth me, and Isabel the Queen.
[*Trumpets sound within*]
The trumpets sound; I must go take my place.   70
Enter the young King [EDWARD III], BISHOP [OF CANTERBURY], CHAMPION,
NOBLES, [*and*] *Queen* [ISABELLA]

Beginning with twenty lines of **soliloquy**, the scene uses the convention that evil characters confide their schemes in the audience. This was so thoroughly accepted that the simple use of the confiding/plotting monologue could be enough to categorise a character as evil. A further indicator is the pervasive use of the first person – 'I' – emphasising his overweening ego, his selfishness and pride. Mortimer rehearses the **syllogistic** logic that has led him to his conclusion that he must have the King killed. Using connections such as 'yet' and 'therefore' as well as 'that' (='so that') displays his carefully logical mental processes. He shows no sign of regret or of any moral qualms whatsoever. The whole piece of reasoning is coldly pragmatic – he is not even angry with Edward any more. In the first line, Mortimer balances his survival against the King's, pivoting the contrast structurally on the central **caesura**. In this way Marlowe's verse images the rhythms of Mortimer's thought. Although his scheme is convoluted, Mortimer explains it lucidly, and translates the problematic Latin sentence as he goes, making its **ambiguous** interpretation clear. Mortimer's logic is that his involvement in the death must be secret in order to avoid punishment later. He goes to great lengths to obscure evidence and so avoid the possibility that responsibility could be traced back to him. Self-satisfaction can be heard in the lines concluding each phase of the argument:
- 'And therefore will I do it cunningly' (line 5)
- 'And we be quit that caused it to be done' (line 16)

- 'Shall he be murdered when the deed is done' (line 20).

Pride in his own plot is evident not only in the words used, but also in the sense of closure provided by the **end-stopped** lines. The death-knell of a *fait accompli* sounds in the repeated 'done'.

Mortimer's reasoning resembles that of a modern detective story, or a lawcourt: he believes that only absolute, demonstrable proof of guilt can trap him. In the closing scene (Scene 25) the young Edward will cut through all that with a single, clear-sighted judgement, based on a much more arbitrary kind of justice.

His plot explained, Mortimer calls for Lightborne by name. 'Lightborne' recalls the name of the devil, Lucifer, and Mortimer's way of calling him may well have reminded the audience of plays where devils were conjured up (such as Marlowe's own *Dr Faustus*). Lightborne has been nearby, probably behind the traverse (a curtained-off alcove at the centre rear of the stage). Suddenly it appears that Mortimer is not in fact in control of every detail: only Lightborne knows the secret of how he will do the murder. For all his English name, Lightborne has foreign connections, having learned the art of secret murder in Naples, in southern Italy (see Themes, on England). Italy had ambiguous connotations for a sixteenth-century English audience, to say the least. On one hand a source of intellectual and artistic sophistication, it was also known as the home of **Machiavelli,** and so stood in people's minds for devilish plots and immoral violence and of the legendary crimes of Lucretia Borgia. It was also connected with the hated 'Popish' religion of Roman Catholicism.

Lightborne's techniques involve unnatural invasions of the victim's body, via the nose, the throat, the ears or the mouth (see Historical Background, on Nature/the Unnatural). Without stating as much, these are contrasted with the more honest, public methods such as stabbing, which leave an identifiable source of death. There are, of course, other orifices as yet unmentioned by Lightborne, which he calls 'a braver way' (meaning 'cleverer' and not 'more courageous'). Mortimer says farewell to Lightborne with the give-away of his intentions characteristic of the stage villain. He accidentally speaks the truth and then retracts it. The words 'never see me more' (line 42) could inform Lightborne of the death planned for him. Lightborne picks up on this, but Mortimer quickly covers his tracks with a plausible lie: 'Unless thou bring me news of Edward's death' (line 44).

Mortimer, again alone on stage, launches into a speech gloating over his own dominating success. It is strongly rhythmic: the first six lines are an almost hypnotic chant of delight and pride. Pride, of course, was widely seen as one of the worst of the Deadly Sins, since it rivalled God. Mortimer has achieved the object of his desire – the highest pinnacle of power. In the cycle of *his* narrative, this is the point from which he will fall. He uses the vocabulary of a tyrant: pleased to be feared rather than loved, and comparing himself with the overbearing schoolmaster Aristarchus. He gloats over his ability to trick the council into believing he is humble like 'a bashful Puritan', and reluctant to take power. This manoeuvre and indeed the whole speech are strongly redolent of Shakespeare's *Richard III*. Dangerously, Mortimer is now far out of control, and plans to do whatever he likes (line 66). This concept of kingship is identical with Edward's at Scene 16, line 3: 'And triumph Edward with his friends uncontrolled'. It also indicates Mortimer's overreaching spirit and imminent fall.

This scene, as so many in *Edward II*, is immensely flexibly staged (see Staging). Mortimer's solitude is varied by the sly arrival of Lightborne from a secret spy-hole. Next, however, he says 'I must go and take my place', but instead of the exit we might have expected, the playwright exercises his control over the stage location and the coronation procession of King Edward III arrives on stage in full splendour. Thus the action comes to Mortimer's location, and not the location to the action.

The coronation will give Edward III confidence and moral power. He will quickly turn out to be a far more effective force for justice than Mortimer anticipates in this extract.

PART FIVE

BACKGROUND

CHRISTOPHER MARLOWE & HIS WORKS

Christopher Marlowe was born in 1564 in Canterbury, Kent and died of a knife wound in Deptford, London on 30 May 1593. His biography can read almost like a work of fiction, with its dramatic moments, its sense of mystery, and its violent early end. Scholars have been fascinated by Marlowe's life, and documents relating to it continue to be discovered. At this distance in time, much of what is suggested about him involves speculation and interpretation.

Marlowe's father was a cobbler, but even so Christopher Marlowe was well educated, attending first the King's School, Canterbury and going on to university studies at Corpus Christi College, Cambridge. Much of the curriculum at Cambridge at that time involved the intensive study of theology and of ancient languages. While still a student at Cambridge, Marlowe travelled abroad on Government business, from which information scholars believe that he was probably spying. In particular he may have infiltrated the (Catholic) Jesuit community at Rheims in France. This could be consistent with the idea that he was a member of the puritan movement, and followed its emphasis on free speech. Alternatively, it is also speculated that Marlowe may have become a Catholic sympathiser and a double agent while in France. This is not so improbable as it might seem, since both the State and powerful members of the nobility certainly did run spy networks throughout the Tudor period, which was fraught with both foreign wars and internal dissent. Marlowe's own contribution to this is probable rather than proven. Especially interesting reading on this topic is Charles Nicholl, *The Reckoning: The Murder of Christopher Marlowe* (Jonathan Cape, 1992).

Marlowe left Cambridge for London in 1587 taking up the profession of playwright, at which he was immediately successful with *Tamburlaine the Great* and its sequel, *Tamburlaine the Great, Part II*. The hero of these plays is a bloodthirsty tyrant, and audiences flocked to see the spectacular battle scenes, and to hear the blood-curdling poetry in the grand style with which Tamburlaine conducted politics as slaughter. Tamburlaine foreshadows Mortimer in *Edward II* as well as Faustus in *Dr Faustus* in his overweening pride and ambition.

The dates of composition of Marlowe's plays are not absolutely certain, and he may have begun writing while still at university. *Dido, Queen of Carthage* probably dates from this early period, followed by the two parts of *Tamburlaine*. *Dr Faustus* was probably written next, in the late 1580s, followed by *The Jew of Malta*, *The Massacre at Paris* and *Edward II* in that order. *Edward II* is thus the last and most maturely constructed.

In addition, Marlowe wrote lyric poetry, translated Ovid's *Amores* and Lucan's *Pharsalia*, and composed 'Hero and Leander', an **epyllion** of great charm.

Marlowe's lifestyle in London after leaving university was that of a single young man who lived amongst a crowd of similar friends, including the playwright Thomas Kyd, and made money as and where he could. His contacts included intellectuals, con-men and spies. While he is reported to have spent time in serious conversations about religion, he also fell foul of the law over brawls on two occasions: in 1589 and in 1592. He had powerful political connections, including the spymaster and Secretary of State to Queen Elizabeth I, Sir Francis Walsingham (died 1590) and his brother Thomas Walsingham.

At the time and shortly after his death contemporaries such as Richard Baines claimed that Marlowe expressed atheistic and seditious views. Baines wrote that 'almost into every company he cometh he persuades men to Atheism, willing them not to be afeared of burglars and hobgoblins, and utterly scorning both god and his ministers'. Baines claimed that Marlowe asserted 'all they that love not tobacco and boys were fools'. Thomas Kyd while under arrest also made accusations against Marlowe. We cannot take this so-called evidence as uncomplicated truth, as it is hearsay and could well have been invented by enemies who wished to discredit Marlowe and his friends.

It is possible that Marlowe's death, whether by accident or murder, was connected with Baines's accusations and the scandal which was about to emerge. Marlowe was invited to a meal at a house in Deptford, at the end of which he was dead from a knife-wound to the eye. The two other men present narrated a story of a quarrel and a scuffle during which this nasty accident occurred, and the coroner was satisfied. Scholars such as Leslie Hotson and Charles Nicholl have been rather more suspicious, seeing Marlowe's death and the subsequent blackening of his reputation as altogether too convenient. J.B. Steane puts the opposite view for seeing these reports of Marlowe as possibly exaggerated, but having some basis in fact: 'As for Marlowe the man, atheist and rebel or not, we have to acknowledge that there is no single piece of evidence that is not hearsay – only that there is a good deal of it, that it is reasonably consistent, and that on the other side there is no single fact or piece of hearsay known to us that will rank as evidence against it' (p. 16).

An output of seven major plays in six years was sufficient to give Marlowe an impressive place amongst the most highly regarded dramatists. His tragically early death at the age of twenty-nine no doubt deprived literature of even greater and more developed works. As Simon Shepherd puts it (reluctantly, for he is not a biographically centred critic) in his Introduction to *Marlowe and the Politics of Elizabethan Theatre* (Harvester, 1986), 'I would suggest that had he lived Marlowe might well have produced a set of texts of an artistic quality that would rival if not excel Shakespeare's' (p. xiii).

LITERARY BACKGROUND

CHRONICLES & HISTORY PLAYS

Edward II uses the tradition of the Chronicle play or **history play** and develops it further. Although available during the Middle Ages, chronicles of English history became increasingly popular through the sixteenth century as part of a widespread urge to define national identity. The Chronicles themselves contained both mythic and factual material – for example Geoffrey of Monmouth's twelfth-century history treated the stories of King Arthur as historical truth, and was still widely read through the sixteenth century. John Bale (1495–1563) had written the first history play, *King John*, in the early sixteenth century and it seems likely that the three parts of *King Henry VI* (by Shakespeare and other collaborators) had been written in some form slightly earlier than *Edward II*, since they were already being performed in 1592. Though these plays are based on histories, it is important to remember that they are creative fictional constructs, and cannot be relied on for historical information. The material on which Marlowe based *Edward II* was principally gathered from Holinshed (Raphael Holinshed's *Chronicles of England, Scotland and Ireland*, editions of which had appeared in 1577 and 1587). It was Marlowe's genius that interpreted and edited the chaotic historical sequence of events in Holinshed into an artistic and powerful narrative. In particular, Marlowe foregrounds personal relationships and presents them as the motivating force behind political events. (See also: Irving Ribner, *The English History Play in the Age of Shakespeare*, Oxford University Press, 1957.)

MARLOWE & THE EARLY SHAKESPEARE

Many critics have noticed resemblances between the works of Marlowe and those produced by Shakespeare in the early 1590s. Discussions are often highly technical, involving detailed linguistic comparisons. There are particular resemblances between *Edward II* and Shakespeare's *Richard II*, and much concentrated study has been devoted to comparisons. Certainly the latter seems to have drawn substantially on the former. It has also been suggested that Shakespeare and Marlowe may have collaborated on some early Shakespearean plays, such as the Henriad, *Titus Andronicus* and *Edward III*. These issues are discussed by Glynne Wickham, *Shakespeare's Dramatic Heritage* (London, 1969), pp. 165–79, and by Wolfgang Clemen, 'Shakespeare and Marlowe', in Clifford Leech & J.M.R. Margeson eds. *Shakespeare 1971* (Toronto, 1972), pp. 123–32.

THE *DE CASIBUS* TRADITION

This Latin phrase, meaning 'of the falls', is based on the Italian writer Boccaccio's 'De Casibus Virorum Illustrium' – 'Of the Falls of Great Men'. It refers to collections of stories of the lives of powerful people who have come to disgrace or poverty or even damnation through their misjudgements or moral failings. The poet John Lydgate translated and invented many such stories in the 1430s. One might reasonably also connect this biographising urge with Plutarch's 'Parallel Lives of the Ancient Grecians and Romans'.

The '*de casibus*' tradition intersects with other popular **topoi**:

- the Dance of Death, in which it is shown **allegorically** that Death comes to everyone regardless of their worldly power. It appeared in poetry and in many illustrations throughout Europe in the late-medieval period. A group of woodcuts by Hans Holbein is probably now the most familiar version.
- the classical concept of the '**tragic** hero': a potentially great man who falls due to a single character flaw.
- Fortune and her wheel. Like the Dance of Death, this involved visual representations as well as written narratives and references. People were envisaged as having a place on this giant wheel, and as it turned they rose and then fell, inexorably. Mortimer claims to control the wheel himself at Scene 21, line 52, and to be subject to it at Scene 25, lines 59–63. The wheel is an image of human helplessness in the face of Fate: a popular tune of the sixteenth century was called 'Fortune my Foe', and there are records of thieves asking to have it played before their executions.

CLASSICAL TRADITION: OVID

Ovid's *Metamorphoses*, (written between the years 1 and 8CE) were tales of fantasy about the transformation of humans or gods into animals, plants or other forms, and were hugely popular in the Early Modern period, when Marlowe was writing. Perceived as elegant, fashionable material, the *Metamorphoses* were used as inspiration for poetry and constituted recognisable points of reference for educated people. Frequently about illicit or perverse sexual desire and sometimes gratification, the stories were often set in a mythic classical landscape. References to Ovid occur in a very focused way in *Edward II*. Much of Gaveston's speech in Scene 1 has a delicate, sensuous quality infused with ideas of control which one might see as 'Ovidian'. By using the story of Actaeon (see notes to Scene 1), Gaveston conveys an impression of decadent sophistication and intellectualism. The same lush atmosphere of sensuality and death can be found in the long narrative poems of the early 1590s such as Marlowe's own **epyllion** 'Hero and Leander' and

Shakespeare's 'Rape of Lucrece' and 'Venus and Adonis'. The perversity of Actaeon's capacity to glimpse the goddess is presented as parallel to Edward's more studied gaze at the boy actor (as imagined by Gaveston), and indicates a kind of eroticism in which desire might have nonstandard objects. Actaeon's glance is punished by death, as is Edward's erotic gaze. Actaeon, as well as the lovers Gaveston and Edward, is destroyed by beings whom he would normally expect to command: the hounds in the former case, and the rebellious lords in the latter.

Other classical references include Hercules and Hylas (Scenes 1 and 4), Plato and Alcibiades (Scene 4) and Achilles and Patroclus (Scene 4).

HISTORICAL BACKGROUND

A **history play** always has a double historical background: the period which it describes and the period in which it is written. It is important to keep these distinct. Perhaps surprisingly, a play such as *Edward II* tells us most about the time in which it was written – that is, the early 1590s. That is the historical background I will refer to here. There is a good discussion of the Chronicles' representation of Edward II in the Introduction to the Revels' Plays edition, pp. 41–66.

ATTITUDES TO HOMOSEXUALITY

Explanations of sixteenth-century sexuality, so different from our own, are made more complex by the anachronistic terms one must use. The term 'homosexual' was not introduced to English until 1897 (OED). The sixteenth century did have words for homosexual lovers: 'minion' (1501), 'ingle' (OED records 1592, but probably in use earlier) and 'catamite' (1593) were all available. For the sake of clarity, sixteenth-century attitudes to activities or feelings which we would now class as homosexual can be divided into the official/judicial on one hand, and those which were commonplace in society as a whole on the other.

Officially, 'sodomy' was considered a crime punishable by death, but the definition of 'sodomy' included heterosexual and animal relations as well as homosexual. It referred broadly to nonprocreative sex. This law was rarely invoked, and probably only in cases where the offence was aggravated by other features such as under-age partners, the use of force, or transgression of class boundaries.

In the mundane world, male-male love affairs and partnerships seem to have been as commonplace as they are today, and as widely accepted. This, of course, makes it harder for historians to examine them, as ordinary behaviour attracts little comment and leaves no obvious record. To find evidence, we have to interpret literary materials, such as Mortimer Senior's speech in Scene 4, lines 387–402, which is tolerant, and Isabella's 'thou corrupts my lord' (Scene 4, line 150) which is denigratory, but imprecise.

NATURE/THE UNNATURAL

The twin concepts of what is 'natural' and what is 'unnatural' recur throughout this play. The sixteenth century read the word 'natural' as a reference to heredity: behaving according to nature meant following one's parents' example. Thus it is 'unnatural' when Edward does not follow the kind of kingship (and masculinity) defined by the example of his dominant and successful father, Edward I.

By an easy extension, any foreign connection could be seen as 'unnatural', simply because it has a different parentage (see Themes, on England). The term is always pejorative, in the same way as being 'kind' (i.e. good to your kin, or relatives) is always positive. When Edward is described as 'unnatural', this refers to a complex of ideas in which one should include:

- disobedience to his father's wishes
- neglecting his upper-class friends and relations, while giving lower-class persons excessive titles
- giving away English titles to a foreigner
- failing to look after his people (the royal relationship with the people was seen as comparable with that of a father to a child, or a lord to his retainers)
- neglecting his wife
- having homosexual affairs
- governing rashly (unlike Edward I).

Examples are numerous: Scene 1, lines 98–9: 'your peers / That naturally would love and honour you,' suggest that Edward has deformed the natural law by alienating the lords. When Pembroke asks 'Can kingly lions fawn on creeping ants', his **allegorical rhetoric** means that the King and nobles (the lions) would have to change their nature to show respect to Gaveston (the ant). Edward, in showing such respect, behaves unnaturally (Scene 4, line 15). Whenever animal comparisons are made in this play, the concept of behaving according to one's 'nature' is invoked. Gaveston, too, desires to step outside his heredity, picturing himself as Caesar (Scene 1, lines 172–3) and as a king (Scene 4, line 27). Even the inanimate world can behave 'naturally', and Edward habitually pictures the unnatural as preferable to separation from Gaveston: 'sooner shall the sea o'erwhelm the land / Than bear the ship that shall transport thee hence' (Scene 1, lines 151–2). Again unnaturally he places his love for Gaveston above his duty to protect 'my land' and the people on it.

It is within a structure supported by 'nature' that feudal duty has its place. This is why the lords can feel that they no longer owe Edward the duty of allegiance, once they see him as unnaturally neglecting them. Their behaviour is also 'unnatural' in that sense of being outside the family-like relationship between noble and king. This informs Isabella's perception 'Unnatural wars, where subjects brave their King' (Scene 11, line 86). Edward's failure of feudal duty, in his threat to see his country destroyed, enables Warwick's judgement 'A desperate and unnatural resolution' (Scene 12, line 33). The same accusation of dereliction of duty combined with class transgression shows in Kent's 'Unnatural King, to slaughter noblemen / And cherish flatterers' (Scene 14, lines 8–9).

THE ARMY

In a period before any standing army was regularly kept there were two main ways to levy troops. In the first method levies of men were made on a geographical basis, assembled in terms of loyalty to their feudal lords. Records were kept in each county detailing the number of men and arms that each town and village was supposed to provide. There is a scene depicting this kind of conscription in Shakespeare's *Henry IV* Part 2. A village in Warwickshire, for example, might have an obligation to provide three men, fully equipped, if the Earl of Warwick should call on them.

The Earl would then fund their keep for the duration of the conflict. If this was in the King's service, the royal treasury would be expected to pay for men, arms, transport and so on. (This explains the row in *Edward II*, Scene 6, over ransoming Mortimer senior, taken prisoner while in the King's service.) In the second method, men might choose to function as mercenaries for whoever employed them. This is why Lancaster considers selling his castles in order to fund an army of rebellion (Scene 1, lines 102–3).

PART SIX

CRITICAL HISTORY & BROADER PERSPECTIVES

EARLY RECEPTION

In the absence of direct evidence, it is commonly claimed that early performances of *Edward II* were popular. Numerous reprintings suggest a large readership in the thirty years after its first publication. Tastes changed, and the play then remained unperformed until William Poel's 1903 production. It has been presented with gradually increasing frequency since then, with Bertolt Brecht opening his own German version in 1924.

The play itself has been used politically to break down barriers against the on-stage representation of homosexuality. Actors of considerable standing including Ian McKellen and Simon Russell Beale have taken on the role of Edward II with notable success.

Critics have found this play especially interesting from a **formal** point of view, as part of the history of the development of English drama. They have discussed whether this is primarily a **history play** (with a political focus) or a **tragedy** (with a personal focus). To look solely at one or the other is now considered to be limiting. D. M Bevington has pointed out that many of the contradictions within the characters stem from Marlowe's use of the **conventions** of the **Morality Play** (see *From 'Mankind' to Marlowe: Growth and Structure in the Popular Drama of Tudor England*). In terms of **dramaturgy**, Marlowe found these conventions impressively enabling. Certainly his management of the techniques of addition and substitution to manoeuvre characters on and off stage while sustaining unbroken action is masterly.

Critics treating the political emphasis have focused on the power-play between a weak king and the powerful barons. Furthermore, the King troubles the barons' view of Englishness as bluff, manly and direct by introducing foreign tastes along with Gaveston. He attacks a hierarchy of power which has worked for generations, and **implicitly** shows how far the feudal system has slipped away from associating strength and competence with formal power. Instead, it is clear that hereditary kingship contains its own problems of weak leadership and what we might now call 'personality politics'.

The barons can only come to terms with this by stepping outside the system of allegiance themselves: a **paradox** which removes them from the moral high ground. The play copes with this by isolating the worst acts of disloyalty in single individuals (Warwick kills Gaveston; Mortimer is responsible for Edward's death). These, in turn, in the manner of all scapegoats, are defined as peculiarly evil or alien to the culture they have served and quickly executed. In this way, disloyalty can be contained and the system of the strong ruler is re-established and preserved through Edward III. This does not, of course, address the inherent flaws that Edward has revealed in the political system.

This kind of reading ignores the personal dimension of the play. Many critics have viewed it as primarily a love story, and focused on the conflicts within Isabella, the sacrifices that Gaveston and Edward make for their love, and so on. Dynamic personal antagonisms and attachments motivate the individual characters. The degree and timing of Isabella's betrayal is of interest. Gaveston's motivation is also contradictory: at times he almost gloats over his power over the King, but at others he expresses genuine affection. Edward's insecure identity (see Themes, on Identity) has attracted analysis and discussion, as has the tragedy of his downfall. Marlowe also succeeds in abandoning the Morality Play's division of subsidiary characters into the absolutely good and the absolutely evil. Instead they all participate in the **mankind figure**'s capacity to be swayed one way and then the other. Kent is a prominent example; Mortimer and Lightborne are notable exceptions. (See Michael Hattaway, *Elizabethan Popular Theatre: Plays in Performance*, Routledge, 1982.)

RECENT CRITICISM

Although this section treats modern criticism as if it can be categorised, in fact there is considerable overlap among the schools of thought treated below.

'QUEER THEORY'

This is the half-playful term for a group of developments which have arisen from the broader area of gender studies. Where the latter considers the cultural construction of concepts of masculinity and femininity, queer theory looks at how gender-constructs can be played with, developed, transgressed or otherwise skewed. Most importantly, it then goes on to consider what meanings are generated by a 'queer' approach to literature. The founding discussion on these issues is Eve Kosowsky Sedgwick, *Between Men: English Literature and Male Homosocial Desire* (Columbia University Press, 1993).

Edward II has at times been treated as a gay icon. It is a play where homosexuality is ingrained in the text in such a way as to be both focused and matter-of-fact: both necessary and ignored. Edward's sexuality is constantly imposed on us by the play, but its significance is equally constantly undercut by disclaimers such as Mortimer's 'Uncle, his wanton humour grieves not me' (Scene 4, line 403). Edward's love for Gaveston collapses the distinctions that the barons wish to sustain: divisions not just between male and female, but also between low and high, English and foreign. These are the contrasts that have formed their world. By ennobling Gaveston (and then Spencer) he demolishes the barons' definition of themselves through their status – he makes noble status as trivial as putting on a costume, or choosing to use a different name. The lords use anger and violence to try to re-establish their definitions. We have heard that the play-acting world contains play-acting violence. The barons' pressure is to make violence real. One could suggest that acting and disguise 'queers' reality by infusing the watchers with a sense of confusion about what is real and what is not, at many levels (see also Textual Analysis, Text 1). Edward has desired a fantasy love – a love expressed in grandiosely **rhetorical** terms. This ultimately becomes a desire for the most real thing available, namely death. Lightborne makes death as 'embodied' and as far from poetry as one could imagine. Yet that word 'imagine' provides another problem, for we in the audience see this ultimate reality *enacted*: it is still not 'real'. So perhaps Edward's world wins, and Mortimer's grip on reality must fade, as he moves towards a death which is an uncertainty 'as a traveller / Goes to discover countries yet unknown' (Scene 25, lines 65–6).

Gregory W. Bredbeck has written about *Edward II* in *Sodomy and Interpretation: Marlowe to Milton* (Cornell, 1991), pp. 48–77. See also Alan Bray, *Homosexuality in Renaissance England* (Columbia University Press, 1982).

PERFORMANCE CRITICISM

This kind of analysis sees the printed playtext, that is normally read and studied, as an incomplete blueprint for an imagined complete form, which, in turn, is achieved in performance. In this theory a play is ephemeral: a highly fluid object of study that vanishes in taking place. Any production is different from every other, and for that matter, if one adds the concept of rapport with the audience to one's definition of a play, every *performance* is a unique event, different from every other. Performance criticism thus reads the *staging* of a play for its meaning, and not just the text. One needs to consider the significance of casting, costume, style and so forth as part of a meaningful system of signs. Portions of the discussion of Characterisation lead towards a performance-based approach to *Edward II*.

A play is a particularly appropriate form in which to play with points of view, as each character adopts his or her own voice. Edward's shaky identity can come to the fore. Both sides in the conflict perform indefensible actions, and more to the point, both are at times identified with stage conventions of immoral or even evil behaviour (see **Vice**). Sympathy therefore shifts, never settles perfectly with any character, leaving audiences uneasy. We want to pity someone who comes to such a horrible end as Edward does, but we also cannot forget how far his tactlessness and lack of insight have led him to his death. We want to feel angry with the aggressors, but they too are understandable in their anxiety, patriotism and in the childishly fiery tempers with which they attempt to cope with the sense of insecurity that Edward amply provides.

STAGING

Marlowe's stage location is entirely flexible: it can represent anywhere and everywhere in rapid succession, and the transitions between these places are not subject to reason. The dramatic convention is that the 'scene' can be anywhere, and the absence of props or realistic scenery makes this feasible. The audience can be trusted to adjust to the sequence of hints that the dialogue gives them regarding location, and to suspend any expectation of realism in regard to staging. It is the interactions between people that matter together with the consequent actions, and the scene only comes into focus as specific place when absolutely necessary. Such an approach to **symbolic** action also makes Marlowe's treatment of time possible, for events can move smoothly onwards eliding the time one might expect to be taken in between. In this play, **natural time** will be hugely compressed to become **stage time**, and there are no gaps in the action in which we might be asked to imagine time passing. Far from it: the action is continuous and fast-paced, with causes and effects running hard on one another's heels. This creates a dazzlingly artistic smoothness of composition and enhances the audience's sense of inevitability, as one event piles on another.

NEW HISTORICISM

New Historicism intersects with Performance Criticism. It is concerned with the ways in which power structures in society are represented in its literary (and other artistic) products. Further, it is concerned with the ways in which such representations are manipulated in order to reinforce power structures and images of society through the **symbolic** codes of display. Based on the work of Barthes and developed by many others, notably Stephen Greenblatt, New Historicism recounts ways in which literature is not 'innocent' or neutral, but politicised and committed to certain, often unspoken, values.

From that point of view one might interpret *Edward II* as echoing some of the anxieties accompanying the debate over Queen Elizabeth's marriage, especially given that both monarchs are gendered ambiguously in their public personae. One reason why she never married was a fear that as a wife she would be obliged to obey her husband (who might well be a foreigner). In *Edward II* we see a king with a highly dominant partner who brings ruin on the kingdom. This is precisely what Elizabeth feared, and it may have been a widespread fear. Secondly, we see a betrayed wife reduced to despair and then to evil: another profound anxiety over any royal marriage. While Elizabeth remained the Virgin

Queen, she could avoid these dangers and claim to be married to her country. Again her behaviour contrasts reassuringly with Edward's, who readily gives away England, sometimes **metaphorically**, sometimes rhetorically. See Stephen Greenblatt, 'Marlowe and the Will to Absolute Play' in *Renaissance Self-Fashioning* (Chicago UP, 1980) and Simon Shepherd, *Marlowe and the Politics of Elizabethan Theatre* (Harvester, 1986).

FEMINISM

It has been said earlier that all social classes are present in the play. That is only true, of course, if one focuses on the masculine world: the female world is largely ignored. Feminist criticism considers the place of women in literature, using concepts and terminology from other areas of criticism such as psychoanalysis. The concepts of 'presence' and 'absence' and of 'speech' and 'silence' are especially important.

Of the women in the play, one is not present at all. We hear of Pembroke's wife as a member of the class of 'pretty wenches' (Scene 9) but her function in the play is merely to distract Pembroke long enough for Warwick to kill Gaveston. (Some compliment may have been intended to the contemporary Earl of Pembroke, whose players performed this play.) Pembroke's wife is thus a silent woman and a sex object, as is Lady Clare, Gaveston's fiancée (and later wife).

Queen Isabella, by contrast, is a powerful stage presence and a politically active figure. Even when we first see her and she is deeply distressed; she is a striking and expressive figure who focuses the attention of everyone around her. In her, sexuality and power are intertwined and she is willing to manipulate each in order to obtain the other. She is dominant, clever and articulate, though ultimately the pawn of Mortimer. We must ask ourselves what the play has to say about women if the only prominent female figure is corrupt and possibly even villainous. She falls into the category of the terrifying Medusa-figure, on to whom men project their fears of female power. But even Isabella is controlled by masculine power: Mortimer silences her abruptly in Scene 17. Her son proves his own dominance, when he has her imprisoned in the Tower, thus containing her literally and **metaphorically** at the close of the play. See Jonathan Dollimore, *Radical Tragedy* (Harvester, 1984).

BIOGRAPHY

Leslie Hotson, *The Death of Christopher Marlowe* (London, 1925)
> This older book was the first really thorough piece of scholarship to cast doubt on the official circumstances of Marlowe's death

Charles Nicholl, *The Reckoning: The Murder of Christopher Marlowe* (Jonathan Cape, 1992)
> A very readable description of Marlowe's London lifestyle, and of the people with whom he associated. Nicholl argues that Marlowe was murdered for political reasons

EDITIONS

Forker, Charles R., ed., *Edward the Second*, by Christopher Marlowe, The Revels Plays (Manchester University Press, 1994)
> The thorough Introduction addresses in greater detail many of the issues raised in thIS Notes

Steane, J. B., ed., *Christopher Marlowe: The Complete Plays* (Penguin, 1969)
> The Introduction offers a clear critical discussion of *Edward II*, of the more conventional type

Wiggins, Martin & Robert Lindsey, eds, Christopher Marlowe, *Edward the Second* (New Mermaids, 1997)
> The edition on which this Note is based

FURTHER COLLECTIONS OF CRITICAL ESSAYS

Leech, Clifford, ed., *Marlowe: A Collection of Critical Essays* (Prentice Hall, 1964)

O'Neil, Judith, ed., *Critics on Marlowe* (University of Miami Press, 1969)

World events	Marlowe's life	Literary events
		1304 Dante, *Divine Comedy*
1307 Edward II accedes to throne of England		
1314 Edward II invades Scotland; Battle of Bannockburn		
1319 Siege of Berwick		
1327 Edward II deposed and murdered; accession of Edward III		
		1341 Petrarch crowned laureate poet in Rome
		1352 (c) Boccaccio, *Decameron*
		1369 Geoffrey Chaucer, *The Book of the Duchess*
		1438 John Lydgate, *The Fall of Princes,* translation of Boccaccio's *De Casibus Virorum Illustrium*
1492 Columbus sets sail for America		
		1513 Niccolò Machiavelli, *The Prince*
		1528 Castiglione, *Book of the Courtier*
		1532 Ariosto, *Orlando Furioso*
1534 Henry VIII breaks with Rome		
1547 Henry VIII (now Protestant) dies; Edward VI (Protestant) accedes		
1553 Edward VI dies; succeeded by Lady Jane Grey for nine days; Mary I (Catholic) accedes		
1556 Archbishop Cranmer burnt at stake		
1558 Mary I dies; Elizabeth I accedes to throne		

World events	Marlowe's life	Literary events
		1562 Lope de Vega, great Spanish dramatist born
		1563 John Bale, author of first history play, *King John*, dies
	1564 Christopher Marlowe born, Canterbury, son of a shoemaker	**1564** William Shakespeare born
1570 Elizabeth I excommunicated by Pope Pius V		
1576 James Burbage builds the first theatre in England, at Shoreditch		
1577 Francis Drake sets out on voyage around the world		**1577** Holinshed's, *Chronicles*
		1580 Sir Philip Sidney, *An Apologie for Poetrie*
1584 Raleigh's sailors land in Virginia	**1584** Awarded BA at Corpus Christi college, Cambridge	
	1587 (pre) Makes a trip to Continent, possibly for espionage	
1587 Mary, Queen of Scots executed	**1587** *Tamberlaine the Great* written by this date	**1587** *Chronicles* republished
		1580s (late) Shakespeare, *Henry VI, Parts 1,2 & 3; Richard III*
1588 Spanish Armada defeated		**1588** Thomas Kyd, *A Spanish Tragedy*
	1589 Involved in a street fight, in which a man was killed, Shoreditch	
	1590 *Tamberlaine* published	**1590** Edmund Spenser, *Faerie Queene (Books I-III)*
1592 Plague closes London theatres	**1592** Deported from the Netherlands for attempting to issue forged coins	
	1593 Killed by Ingram Frizer in pub brawl	

CHRONOLOGY

World events	Marlowe's life	Literary events
	1594 *Tragedie of Dido, Queen of Carthage;* **Edward II** published	**1594** Shakespeare, *Titus Andronicus*
	1595 *The Passionate Pilgim* includes his poem 'Come live with me and be my love'	**1595 (pre)** Shakespeare, *Two Gentlemen of Verona, The Taming of the Shrew, Love's Labour's Lost* probably written
		1595 (c) Shakespeare, *Romeo and Juliet*; death of William Painter, author of *Palaces of Pleasure*
1596 English raid on Cadiz		**1596-8** First performance of Shakespeare, *A Midsummer Night's Dream; Much Ado About Nothing* printed; *As You Like It* mentioned
1598-9 Globe theatre built at Southwark	**1598** *Hero and Leander* published	
		1600-1 Shakespeare, *Hamlet*
1603 Death of Elizabeth I and accession of James Stuart		
	1604 *Dr Faustus* published	**1604** Shakespeare, *Othello*
1605 Discovery of Guy Fawkes's plot		**1605** Shakespeare, *King Lear;* Cervantes, *Don Quijote de la Mancha*
		1606 Shakespeare, *Macbeth*
1610 William Harvey discovers circulation of blood		
1612 Last burning of heretics in England		
		1616 Shakespeare dies
		1622 Molière, French dramatist, born
	1633 *The Jew of Malta* published	

allegory (allegorical) a figurative narrative or description, conveying a veiled moral meaning; the representation within a narrative of abstract concepts by characters bearing their names; thus an extended metaphor or a sustained personification

alliteration a sequence of repeated consonantal sounds in a stretch of language. The matching consonants are usually at the beginning of words or stressed syllables. In Middle English verse alliteration was used with structuring effect, and perceived as a variety of rhyme. It is less common to alliterate on vowels, though that can happen, e.g. 'Edward, England's scourge' (Scene 13, line 38). The latter technique is also called assonance

ambiguous having two or more possible meanings. The reader should notice both meanings at once, rather than choosing one. Most puns are based on ambiguities

ambivalence (ambivalent) ambiguity of feeling; the co-existence of two different attitudes to the same object

aphorism a brief, witty and apt saying

archetype (archetypal) the recurrent themes, images, patterns and characters which occur in all literatures as well as in myths and even dreams. They have a special power to intensify meaning

argument a logically reasoned construction in which premisses are analysed to arrive at a conclusion. The validity of an argument has nothing to do with its truth, since that depends on the accuracy of the premisses

aside(s) a remark made on stage which is not intended to be heard by other characters on stage, but is heard by the audience. It conveys information about feelings and plans

assonance the correspondence or near correspondence of the vowel sounds in two nearby words

ballad rhythms (ballad metre) a four-lined stanza of alternate four-stress and three-stress lines, usually roughly iambic

bathos (bathetic) (Greek 'deep') a ludicrous descent from the elevated treatment of a subject to the ordinary and dull

blank verse unrhymed iambic pentameter

caesura a clear break in the middle of a line of verse

carnival a literary phenomenon described by the Russian critic Mikhail Bakhtin, especially in his work *Rabelais and his World* (1965). According to him some writers use their works as an outlet for the spirit of carnival, of popular festivity and *misrule*. They 'subvert' the literary culture of the ruling classes, undermining its claim to moral monopoly. Such forms and genres are open and 'dialogic'. They allow multiple points of view to co-exist and are valued for their availability to 'plural' interpretations

closure the impression of completeness and finality achieved by the ending of some literary works or parts of literary works

commonplace a well-known saying, or possibly a recurrent motif or subject in literature

convention (conventional) certain standard, common features of the particular kind of literature in question. Often the conventions of a particular form are a consequence of its nature. Drama, for example, cannot exist without certain radical conventions: we watch a play in silence and pretend that the stage in front of us is a room, a battlefield, a forest or whatever. Stock characters in drama or the novel, such as the boastful soldier, the bohemian student or the fair young heroine are also conventions. Recurring elements, whether of technique or subject matter, in all kinds of literature turn into the conventions of that form which new authors may copy, alter or reject

couplet a pair of consecutive lines of poetry which rhyme together

de casibus (Latin) 'of the falls'. This is short for *The Falls of Princes*, a group of tales which tell how various kings, emperors and so on met their death. Translated from the popular Latin text into English by John Lydgate, both the stories and the theme remained popular for centuries. They tend to make much of the proverb 'pride goes before a fall', and also connect with the awareness prompted by the 'Dance of Death' image, that all human beings must die, regardless of their original status in life

despair in the Early Modern period, despair meant loss of faith in God, and was signified by suicide. Suicide and despair were often treated as synonymous

diction the choice of words; the kind of vocabulary used

doubled two roles performed by one actor

dramatic irony a feature of many plays: it occurs when the development of the plot allows the audience more information about what is happening than some of the characters themselves have

dramaturgy the practice and theory of drama; the practical skill the dramatist shows in constructing a play

dumb show a common feature of Elizabethan theatre, this was a mimed version of the plot which was to follow

elements the four elements of medieval science, medicine and philosophy were earth, air, water and fire. They were part of a complex system of correspondences in which every part of the natural world had an affiliation to one of them, or to a combination of them. They are related to the system of the 'humours' which supposedly governed personality and somatic types

emblem a symbolic picture which, though often obscure, could be interpreted in some detail. Books of emblems such as Whitney's *Choice of Emblems* were extremely popular during the sixteenth and seventeenth centuries

end-stopped refers to those lines of verse in which the end of the line coincides with the conclusion of a sentence, or the strongly marked end of a phrase. End-stopped lines create a sense of finality

enjambment a line of poetry in which the sentence continues into the next line without any pause being necessary to clarify the grammar

episodic denoting a narrative which is written in the simple form of a series of more or less separable or discrete episodes or incidents, rather than a complicated or involved plot

epithet an adjective or adjectival phrase which describes a special quality or attribute

epyllion (Greek 'little poem') a short narrative poem or 'brief epic', in fashion through the 1590s

fatalist a believer in the theory of predestination: that one's future is already determined by outside forces

form (formal) the conventional pattern or shape to which one expects each example of a genre to conform in order to classify it as part of the genre. Any repeated element will give a sense of pattern which can be considered an aspect of form

generalisation a large and all-encompassing idea or statement, as opposed to 'particularisation', the study of detailed fragments. To generalise is to utter general truths which apply to all relevant cases. It is difficult to generalise adequately and validly on any subject, and so the word has acquired a common pejorative force: to say that a statement is 'just a generalisation' is to imply that it is untrue in many of the cases in which it is supposed to apply

history play a kind of play especially fashionable in the late sixteenth century which based its plot on the historical records, such as Holinshed, sometimes treating the historical record with considerable artistic licence. Such plays include Shakespeare's two great tetralogies: the three *Henry VI* plays followed by *Richard III,* and the later group, *Richard II, Henry IV* Parts 1 and 2 and *Henry V*. Writers of history plays included Peele and Greene, and many others. Marlowe's *Edward II* is a good example of a history play

Holinshed Holinshed, *Chronicles of England, Scotland and Ireland* (1587). The rather bald information in this list of events from English history became the basis for *Edward II* and for numerous other plays, called the 'chronicle plays' or 'history plays

homily (homilies) whether spoken or written, a homily is a sermon-like discourse or short lecture intended to be morally edifying

hubris (hubristic) the self-indulgent confidence that causes a tragic hero to ignore the decrees, laws and warnings of the gods, and therefore defy them to bring about his or her downfall

hyperbole (hyperbolic) overstatement or extreme exaggeration

iambic pentameter verse constructed of lines containing five 'iambs'. An 'iamb' is a sequence of one unstressed syllable followed by one stressed syllable

imagery in its narrowest sense an 'image' is a word-picture, a description of some visible scene or object. More commonly, however, 'imagery' refers to the figurative language in a piece of literature (metaphors and similes); or all the words which refer to objects and qualities which appeal to the senses and feelings

implicit what is implied or suggested but not expressed outright

irony irony consists of saying one thing while meaning another, in an understated way. Irony that is overdone becomes sarcasm

macaronic mixing two (or more) languages together, a common habit in medieval lyric, where the verse might be in English and the refrain in Latin. It can have a satirical effect

Machiavelli (Machiavel) Niccolò Machiavelli (1469–1527); an Italian writer whose work *The Prince* earned him a reputation in England for political cunning and unscrupulous behaviour. Based on his name an evil plotter called the Machiavel or Machevil developed as a stage character

mankind figure the central character in a Morality Play; representative of the ordinary human existence of each of us

memento mori reminder of death (and hence of the need to live a virtuous life). It often took the form of a skull, but in *Edward II* the Mower fills this function

metaphor (metaphorical) a metaphor goes further than a comparison between two different things or ideas by fusing them together: one thing is described as being another thing, thus 'carrying over' all its associations

metonym(ic) a figure of speech whereby a part of something is taken to be the whole. Thus 'blades' can mean 'swords'

misrule (see carnival) inversion of authority such that foolish laws are to be followed

Morality Play an allegory where the forces of good and evil and a Christian moral lesson concerning salvation are dramatised with simplicity and vigour. Many Morality Plays contained a character called the Vice, a half-comic, half-evil tempter

Mystery Play dramatisation of the Old and New Testaments which evolved steadily from about the tenth century onwards. By the fourteenth century elaborate cycles had developed, played in summer during the Feast of Corpus Christi, with each guild (*mysterium*) responsible for a biblical episode. Each scene was presented on a waggon which could be moved around the city. The verse is rough and vigorous, but the later plays show a strong sense of character and psychology

natural time real time

Ovid (Ovidian) Roman author who wrote the *Amores* and the *Metamorphoses*, mythic stories of magic, love and shape-shifting. Ovidian means in the style of Ovid

paradox an apparently self-contradictory statement or one that seems in conflict with all logic and opinion; yet lying behind the superficial absurdity is a meaning or truth

parody an imitation of a specific work of literature or style, devised so as to ridicule its characteristic features

personification (to personify) a variety of figurative or metaphoric language in which things or ideas are treated as if they were human beings, with human attributes and feelings

polysyllables words of several syllables, usually three or more

proleptically a rhetorical term referring to an anticipation of future events in narratives

prose (prosaic) any piece of language that is not patterned by the regularity of some kind of metre. It is contrasted with verse, which contains some element of repetition, creating a pattern

puritan *not* the picture that we have of a puritan. In the sixteenth century puritans were merely adherents to a particular kind of Protestantism. They were known for humility

rhetoric the art of speaking (and writing) effectively so as to persuade an audience. Rhetoric was the subject of several textbooks by Greek and Roman scholars, including Aristotle and Cicero, and was studied at universities during the Middle Ages and Renaissance

rhetorical question a question asked not for the sake of enquiry, but for emphasis: the writer or speaker expects the reader or audience to be totally convinced about the appropriate reply

satire (satirically) literature which exhibits or examines vice and folly and makes them appear ridiculous or contemptible. Satire differs from the comic in having a purpose: it is directed against a person or a type, and it is usually morally censorious. It uses laughter to attack its objects, rather than for mere evocation of mirth or pleasure

soliloquy a curious but fascinating dramatic convention, which allows a character in a play to speak directly to the audience, as if thinking aloud about motives, feelings and decisions. Part of the convention is that a soliloquy provides accurate access to the character's innermost thoughts: we learn more about the character than could ever be gathered from the action of the play alone

stage time the space of time represented on the stage: in the case of *Edward II*, it is twenty years

stichomythia dialogue in which the speakers alternate, each speaker having one line at a time

syllogism (syllogistic argument) a method of argument in logic, in the form of two propositions called premisses which allow a third proposition to be made: the conclusion. Needless to say, the truth of the conclusion is entirely dependent on the truth of the premisses

symbol (symbolic) something which represents something else (often an idea or quality) by analogy or association. Thus white, lion and rose commonly symbolise or represent innocence, courage and beauty. Such symbols exist by convention and tradition. Writers use these conventional symbols but they also invent and create their own

syntax the grammatical arrangement of words in a sentence

theatre-in-the-round theatre arranged in such a way as to allow the audience to surround the acting space on all sides (instead of the conventional face-to-face confrontation between players and audience)

theme (thematic) the abstract subject of a work; its central idea or ideas, which may or may not be explicit or obvious. A text may contain several themes or thematic interests

topos (pl. topoi) (Greek 'place') a common or recurrent motif in literature. Broadly equivalent to the commonplace

tragedy one of the most discussed genres in literature. Basically a tragedy traces the career and downfall of an individual and shows in this downfall both the capacities and the limitations of human life. The protagonist may be superhuman, a monarch or, in the modern age, an ordinary person. Some of the essential quality of tragedy seems to include an element of the scapegoat or sacrifice (implicit in tragedy's original Greek meaning of 'goat song'). In English literature the Elizabethan and Jacobean periods are the great age of tragedy.

Vice the principal tempter and agent of the devil in a Morality Play. His stage business includes: changing his name; making plots and lying; cowardice; and beating his followers with a wooden sword or dagger. The word 'hypocrisy' is frequently associated with the Vice

Jill Barker was educated at the Ipswich Girls' Grammar School (Queeensland) and at the Australian National University. She has an MA and PhD in English Literature from the University of Warwick. She is now a Senior Lecturer at the University of Luton, with special interests in feminist and psychoanalytic interpretations of sixteenth-century dramatic literature and dialogues. Her published work includes reviews of editions of Shakespeare for *The Year's Work in English Studies*, book chapters on psychoanalytic literary theory, and articles on the representation of women in Shakespeare.

York Notes Advanced (£3.99 each)

Margaret Atwood
Cat's Eye

Margaret Atwood
The Handmaid's Tale

Jane Austen
Mansfield Park

Jane Austen
Persuasion

Jane Austen
Pride and Prejudice

Alan Bennett
Talking Heads

William Blake
Songs of Innocence and of Experience

Charlotte Brontë
Jane Eyre

Emily Brontë
Wuthering Heights

Angela Carter
Nights at the Circus

Geoffrey Chaucer
The Franklin's Prologue and Tale

Geoffrey Chaucer
The Miller's Prologue and Tale

Geoffrey Chaucer
Prologue To the Canterbury Tales

Geoffrey Chaucer
The Wife of Bath's Prologue and Tale

Samuel Taylor Coleridge
Selected Poems

Joseph Conrad
Heart of Darkness

Daniel Defoe
Moll Flanders

Charles Dickens
Great Expectations

Charles Dickens
Hard Times

Emily Dickinson
Selected Poems

John Donne
Selected Poems

Carol Ann Duffy
Selected Poems

George Eliot
Middlemarch

George Eliot
The Mill on the Floss

T.S. Eliot
Selected Poems

F. Scott Fitzgerald
The Great Gatsby

E.M. Forster
A Passage to India

Brian Friel
Translations

Thomas Hardy
The Mayor of Casterbridge

Thomas Hardy
The Return of the Native

Thomas Hardy
Selected Poems

Thomas Hardy
Tess of the d'Urbervilles

Seamus Heaney
Selected Poems from Opened Ground

Nathaniel Hawthorne
The Scarlet Letter

Kazuo Ishiguro
The Remains of the Day

Ben Jonson
The Alchemist

James Joyce
Dubliners

John Keats
Selected Poems

Christopher Marlowe
Doctor Faustus

Arthur Miller
Death of a Salesman

John Milton
Paradise Lost Books I & II

Toni Morrison
Beloved

Sylvia Plath
Selected Poems

Alexander Pope
Rape of the Lock and other poems

William Shakespeare
Antony and Cleopatra

William Shakespeare
As You Like It

William Shakespeare
Hamlet

William Shakespeare
King Lear

William Shakespeare
Measure for Measure

William Shakespeare
The Merchant of Venice

William Shakespeare
A Midsummer Night's Dream

William Shakespeare
Much Ado About Nothing

William Shakespeare
Othello

William Shakespeare
Richard II

William Shakespeare
Romeo and Juliet

William Shakespeare
The Taming of the Shrew

William Shakespeare
The Tempest

William Shakespeare
Twelfth Night

William Shakespeare
The Winter's Tale

George Bernard Shaw
Saint Joan

Mary Shelley
Frankenstein

Jonathan Swift
Gulliver's Travels and A Modest Proposal

Alfred, Lord Tennyson
Selected Poems

Alice Walker
The Color Purple

Oscar Wilde
The Importance of Being Earnest

Tennessee Williams
A Streetcar Named Desire

John Webster
The Duchess of Malfi

Virginia Woolf
To the Lighthouse

W.B. Yeats
Selected Poems

FUTURE TITLES IN THE YORK NOTES SERIES

Jane Austen
Emma

Jane Austen
Sense and Sensibility

Samuel Beckett
Waiting for Godot and *Endgame*

Louis de Bernières
Captain Corelli's Mandolin

Charlotte Brontë
Villette

Caryl Churchill
Top Girls and *Cloud Nine*

Charles Dickens
Bleak House

T.S. Eliot
The Waste Land

Thomas Hardy
Jude the Obscure

Homer
The Iliad

Homer
The Odyssey

Aldous Huxley
Brave New World

D.H. Lawrence
Selected Poems

Christopher Marlowe
Edward II

George Orwell
Nineteen Eighty-four

Jean Rhys
Wide Sargasso Sea

William Shakespeare
Henry IV Pt I

William Shakespeare
Henry IV Part II

William Shakespeare
Macbeth

William Shakespeare
Richard III

Tom Stoppard
Arcadia and *Rosencrantz and Guildenstern are Dead*

Virgil
The Aeneid

Jeanette Winterson
Oranges are Not the Only Fruit

Tennessee Williams
Cat on a Hot Tin Roof

Metaphysical Poets

OTHER TITLES

GCSE and equivalent levels (£3.50 each)

Maya Angelou
I Know Why the Caged Bird Sings

Jane Austen
Pride and Prejudice

Alan Ayckbourn
Absent Friends

Elizabeth Barrett Browning
Selected Poems

Robert Bolt
A Man for All Seasons

Harold Brighouse
Hobson's Choice

Charlotte Brontë
Jane Eyre

Emily Brontë
Wuthering Heights

Shelagh Delaney
A Taste of Honey

Charles Dickens
David Copperfield

Charles Dickens
Great Expectations

Charles Dickens
Hard Times

Charles Dickens
Oliver Twist

Roddy Doyle
Paddy Clarke Ha Ha Ha

George Eliot
Silas Marner

George Eliot
The Mill on the Floss

Anne Frank
The Diary of Anne Frank

William Golding
Lord of the Flies

Oliver Goldsmith
She Stoops To Conquer

Willis Hall
The Long and the Short and the Tall

Thomas Hardy
Far from the Madding Crowd

Thomas Hardy
The Mayor of Casterbridge

Thomas Hardy
Tess of the d'Urbervilles

Thomas Hardy
The Withered Arm and other Wessex Tales

L.P. Hartley
The Go-Between

Seamus Heaney
Selected Poems

Susan Hill
I'm the King of the Castle

Barry Hines
A Kestrel for a Knave

Louise Lawrence
Children of the Dust

Harper Lee
To Kill a Mockingbird

Laurie Lee
Cider with Rosie

Arthur Miller
The Crucible

Arthur Miller
A View from the Bridge

Robert O'Brien
Z for Zachariah

Frank O'Connor
My Oedipus Complex and Other Stories

George Orwell
Animal Farm

J.B. Priestley
An Inspector Calls

J.B. Priestley
When We Are Married

Willy Russell
Educating Rita

Willy Russell
Our Day Out

J.D. Salinger
The Catcher in the Rye

William Shakespeare
Henry IV Part 1

William Shakespeare
Henry V

William Shakespeare
Julius Caesar

William Shakespeare
Macbeth

William Shakespeare
The Merchant of Venice

William Shakespeare
A Midsummer Night's Dream

William Shakespeare
Much Ado About Nothing

William Shakespeare
Romeo and Juliet

William Shakespeare
The Tempest

William Shakespeare
Twelfth Night

George Bernard Shaw
Pygmalion

Mary Shelley
Frankenstein

R.C. Sherriff
Journey's End

Rukshana Smith
Salt on the Snow

John Steinbeck
Of Mice and Men

Robert Louis Stevenson
Dr Jekyll and Mr Hyde

Jonathan Swift
Gulliver's Travels

Robert Swindells
Daz 4 Zoe

Mildred D. Taylor
Roll of Thunder, Hear My Cry

Mark Twain
Huckleberry Finn

James Watson
Talking in Whispers

Edith Wharton
Ethan Frome

William Wordsworth
Selected Poems

A Choice of Poets

Mystery Stories of the Nineteenth Century including The Signalman

Nineteenth Century Short Stories

Poetry of the First World War

Six Women Poets

NOTES